1

Table of Contents

Introduction

The Georgia Assessment for the Certification of Educators (GACE): Early Childhood Education Exam is designed to prepare elementary teachers (grades P-5) for the classroom by ensuring that they have a strong knowledge base in the content areas that they will be expected to teach. These content areas are tested via two subtests.

The Test at a Glance

Test	Subtest I (001)	Subtest II (002)	Combined Test (501)
Format	75 multiple choice and 2 constructed-response questions	75 multiple choice questions	Subtests I and II taken in a single session
Topics	• Reading and Language Arts (50%) • Social Studies (25%) • Analysis (Constructed-Response: 25%)	• Mathematics (53%) • Science (30%) • Health Education, Physical Education, and the Arts (17%)	See Subtests I and II at left
Time	2.5 hours with instructions, 2 hours of actual testing time	2.5 hours with instructions, 2 hours of actual testing time	5 hours with instructions, 4 hours of actual testing time
Method	Computer-based	Computer-based	Computer-based

Each of these subtests has multiple topics that will be explored in the rest of this guide.

Reading and Language Arts

Reading and Language Arts are foundational for student success. Students develop skills in reading, writing, and speaking that demonstrate comprehension of written and spoken texts, a command of the mechanics of the English language, and critical thinking skills.

Test Structure

The Reading and Language Arts section makes up 50% of Subtest I. Within Reading and Language Arts, there are five major subcategories with which you must be familiar:

A. Literary and Informational Texts

B. Literacy Development, Fluency, and Comprehension

C. Writing and Research

D. Speaking, Listening, and Presenting

E. Grammar and Vocabulary

Each subcategory is divided into topics, which state the skills you must be able to demonstrate on the exam.

Literary and Informational Texts

There are many types of literary and informational texts available for children. Teachers must be prepared to help children learn to select, comprehend, and analyze these texts.

Topics Addressed:

1. Promoting Comprehension of Literary and Informational Texts
2. Types of Literature
3. Elements of Non-Fiction
4. Elements of Fiction
5. Elements of Poetry
6. Literary Terms

Comprehension is the ability to understand read content, process it, and think about it critically. Comprehension takes reading beyond fluency— which just requires words to be pronounced correctly and fluidly—and into a process in which the words take on deeper meaning.

Factors Affecting Reading Comprehension

There are many factors that affect a child's ability to comprehend written text. These include:

- Background knowledge

- Fluency

- Vocabulary

- Comprehension skills

- Use of comprehension strategies

- Motivation

- Structures and features of the text

Types of Reading Comprehension

The three major types of reading comprehension are literal, inferential, and evaluative comprehension.

1. **Literal comprehension** is understanding of the meaning of the words in a passage. This can include tasks like:
   - Stating the main idea of a passage
   - Identifying the topic sentence of a passage
   - Identifying supporting details

2. **Inferential comprehension** is using information explicitly stated in the passage to determine information that is not stated.
   - Making predictions

- Identifying implicit relationships such as compare and contrast; cause and effect
- Inferring implicit meanings

3. **Evaluative comprehension** involves analysis and/or making judgments about the information presented in the text. This can include tasks like:
   - Drawings conclusions based on evidence in the text
   - Determining the author's purpose
   - Distinguishing fact from opinion
   - Making connections between the text and other sources or situations

Promoting Reading Comprehension

There are many strategies students can employ to increase their reading comprehension. Here are several common ones:

- Annotating texts
- Drawing on prior knowledge to make inferences, make connections, and draw conclusions (also called inferential reading)
- Metacognition—awareness of one's own knowledge; self-monitoring to assess progress, identify difficulties, and employ strategic problem-solving
- Multi-pass strategies such as SQ3R (Survey, Question, Read, Recite, Review)
- Pre- and post-reading exercises such as K-W-L (Know, Want to Know, Learned)
- Summarizing
- Using graphic organizers
- Think-alouds
- Recognizing story structure

There are many types of literature. They fall under two general categories—fiction and non-fiction. **Fiction** is material that not an accurate account of real people and events but rather is imagined by the author. **Non-fiction** is material that is presented as being factual and accurate.

The major forms of fiction and non-fiction literature include, but are not limited to, those listed in the chart that follows:

Fiction	Non-Fiction
• Drama (play)- a piece meant for performance, where the story is presented through dialogue • Novel- a book-length narrative that presents its characters and plot with a degree of realism • Poetry- literature written in verse • Short story- a brief work of narrative prose	• Autobiography- an account of the author's own life • Biography- an account of another person's life • Diary (or journal)- a dated, personal record of events over a period of time • Essay- a short piece intended to express an author's point of view on a topic • Letter- written correspondence from one person to another • Textbook-a book used to study a particular subject

Genres of Children's Literature

Literature for children is written in many different genres. The chart below shows some of the major ones.

Genre	Description
Allegory	Story in which the characters and events represent ideas or concepts
Drama (play)	A piece meant for performance, where the story is presented through dialogue
Fable	A short story with a moral lesson
Fantasy	Stories involving make-believe that often occur in imaginative realms with creatures or powers that do not exist in real life
Folktale	A story passed down through oral traditions
Historical fiction	Story that takes place in the past and is realistic for that time period
Myth	A story created to explain natural or social phenomena
Non-fiction	Factual information
Parable	A short story used to teach a moral lesson
Poetry	Stories or ideas expressed through verse
Picture book	Illustrated stories where the text and pictures are interdependent
Realistic fiction	Fiction that takes place in the contemporary "real world" with characters and situations that are believable
Science fiction	Story created by extending scientific ideas to imaginary, though logical, conclusions; often set in the future
Tall tale	An exaggerated story, usually about a real person

Types of Non-Fiction

Non-fiction writing can be classified as informational, persuasive, or functional.

Informational texts are meant to teach the reader facts about a subject.

Examples:

- Biography or autobiography
- Textbook
- Encyclopedia

Persuasive texts are meant to convince the audience of a point of view.

Examples:

- Editorial
- Persuasive essay

Functional texts provide instructions for the reader.

Examples:

- How-to guide
- Instruction manual

Structures of Non-Fiction Texts

Informational (non-fiction) texts typically have structural components that can help students to comprehend the material and to locate specific information they need. These structural features may include:

- Table of contents
- Glossary
- Index
- Bibliography
- Headings
- Outlines
- Key terms underlined or in bold print
- Graphic components such as illustrations, photographs, charts, graphs, or tables

Teaching students about these textual features can help them to better understand the information presented in the text. These structures are in place to help the reader to summarize and synthesize the information. Some techniques for familiarizing students with these structures are:

- Having students preview these features of the text before reading
- Having a text "scavenger hunt" to locate text features
- Using these features (especially headings and key terms) as the basis for outlines or graphic organizers

The major elements of fiction include setting, theme, plot, character, and point of view.

Setting

The setting is when and where the story takes place. This can be a real or imagined place and time period. The setting is introduced earlier in the story.

Theme

The theme is the underlying idea of a story. A theme may be a message the author is trying to convey, a lesson learned by a character in the story, or a universal truth.

Plot

The plot is made up of the events in the story. There are five parts to a plot:

1. Introduction- the characters, setting, and necessary background information are introduced
2. Rising action- the story becomes more complex and the conflict is introduced
3. The types of conflict are *man vs. man, man vs. self, man vs. nature, man vs. society,* and *man vs. fate*.
4. Climax- the height of the conflict and turning point of the story
5. Falling action- the conflict begins to resolve itself
6. Resolution- the conflict is resolved and the story concludes

Characters

Characters are the people (or sometimes animals or objects) who participate in a story. The two main types of characters are the **protagonist** (the main character or hero) and the **antagonist** (the character that works against the protagonist).

Point of View

Point of view refers to the perspective from which the narration takes place. It addresses who is telling the story (the narrator).

Main Types of Narrators:

- First person- ones of the characters tells the story from his or her own perspective; uses "I"
- Third person- the story is told by an outside voice who is not one of the characters
- Omniscient- a third person narrator who knows everything about all of the characters, including their inner thoughts and feelings.
- Limited omniscient- a third person narrator who only knows the inner thoughts and feelings of one specific character

Poetry is a form of creative literature written in verse.

Types of Poetry

Poetry can take many forms, several of which are listed in the chart below:

Form	Definition
Acrostic	A poem in which the first letter of each line forms a word when read from top to bottom
Ballad	A poem narrating a story in stanzas, often quatrains
Blank Verse	Poetry that is metered but not rhymed
Cinquain	A five line poem with specified syllabic emphasis, depending on the type of cinquain
Concrete	A poem written into a familiar shape relating to the poem's meaning
Elegy	A poem about someone's death
Epic	A long poem about the adventures of a hero
Free Verse	Poetry that is neither rhymed nor metered
Haiku	A Japanese form of poetry that contains three lines of 5, 7, and 5 syllables, in that order
Limerick	A humorous five-line poem with a rhyme scheme of AABBA
Lyric	A poem expressing personal emotions
Ode	A lyric poem addressed to a particular subject, which often contains lofty imagery
Sonnet	A fourteen-line poem

Poetry Terms and Devices

Poetry also has its own unique vocabulary of terms, including techniques that poets employ in creating their works. The chart on the following pages lists several of the major elements used in various forms of poetry.

Term	Definition	Example	
Alliteration	Repetition of a beginning consonant sound	"Peter Piper picked a peck of pickled peppers."	
Assonance	Repetition of vowel sounds	"As I was going to St. Ives, I met a man with seven wives."	
Consonance	Repetition of consonant sounds anywhere in the words	"Hickory, Dickory, Dock, The mouse ran up the clock. The clock struck one, The mouse ran down. Hickory, Dickory, Dock."	
Foot	One unit of meter	*Type of Foot*	*Definition*
		Iambic	Unstressed syllable followed by a stressed syllable
		Trochaic	Stressed syllable followed by an unstressed syllable
		Spondaic	Two stressed syllables in a row
		Pyrrhic	Two unstressed syllables in a row
		Anapestic	Two unstressed syllables followed by a stressed syllable
		Dactylic	Stressed syllable followed by two unstressed syllables
Meter	The rhythm of a poem, dependent on the number of syllables and how they are accented		
Mood	A poem's feeling or atmosphere		
Repetition	Using a word or phrase more than once for rhythm or emphasis	"Show men dutiful? Why, so didst thou: seem they grave and learned? Why, so didst thou: come they of noble family? Why, so didst thou: seem they religious? Why, so didst thou."	

Term	Definition	Example	
Rhyme	The repetition of ending word sounds; can be *internal rhyme* (within a line) or *end rhyme* (the words at the end of the lines rhyme with each other)	Internal rhyme: "Jack <u>Sprat</u> could eat no <u>fat</u>." End rhyme: "Little Miss <u>Muffet</u> Sat on a <u>tuffet</u>"	
Rhythm	The pattern of sounds with a poem		
Stanza	Groups of lines of poetry; named for how many lines they contain	*Name*	*# of Lines*
		Couplet	2
		Triplet	3
		Quatrain	4
		Quintain	5
		Sestet	6
		Septet	7
		Octane	8
Verse	A line of metered poetry; named for the number of feet per line	*Name*	*# of Feet*
		Monometer	1
		Dimeter	2
		Trimeter	3
		Tetrameter	4
		Pentameter	5
		Hexameter	6
		Heptameter	7
		Octometer	8

Literary Terms

Literature employs devices to convey meaning through the written word.

Term	Definition	Example
Alliteration	Repetition of a beginning consonant sound	The lonesome lady left one last, long, look for her love.
Flashback	An interruption in the chronology of a story that takes the narrative back in time from its current point	The novel *Frankenstein* by Mary Shelley is told largely in flashbacks as Dr. Frankenstein recounts his story for a sea captain.
Foreshadowing	An advanced warning or clue as to what is to come later in a story	The witches in Shakespeare's *Macbeth* foreshadow the events to come.
Hyperbole	Exaggeration for emphasis	I'm so hungry I could eat a whole elephant!
Idiom	A phrase that has come to have a different meaning through usage than the meanings of its individual words	Something easy is said to be "a piece of cake."
Imagery	Descriptive writing that appeals to the senses	The rich aroma of coffee drifted through the air, bringing warmth on a bitter January morning.
Metaphor	A comparison between two things that does not use "like" or "as"	He is a chicken.
Onomatopoeia	Words that convey sounds	Buzz, crackle, pop, bang
Oxymoron	Combining two words with opposite meanings	Jumbo shrimp
Personification	Giving human characteristics to nonhuman things	The leaves danced as the wind whistled through the trees.
Simile	A comparison between two things that uses "like" or "as"	Cool as a cucumber

Literacy Development, Fluency, and Comprehension

Language development is a gradual and complex process that begins long before students enter school. In order to support students' further language development, teachers should have a thorough understanding of how language is acquired and how to reach students at varying levels of development.

Topics Addressed:

1. Reading Development
2. Orthographic Development
3. The Role of Fluency

Emergent Literacy

There is important language development that occurs even before a child can read or write words. This is known as **emergent literacy**. These skills are developed from birth and include listening, speaking, memory, recognizing pattern and rhyme, print awareness, critical thinking, and the development of the fine motor skills necessary for writing.

The Role of Oral Language Development in Emergent Literacy

Oral language plays an important role in emergent literacy. Linguistic awareness—the ability to understand sound structures within language—is an essential oral language skill. In order to one day be able to read and write, children need to be able to hear the ways in which language is separated into parts. As they listen to oral language, they begin to recognize similar sounds, rhymes, and, eventually, syllables. Being able to not only recognize but also produce these word parts and patterns orally is an important early step in emergent literacy. Early exposure to frequent language with a wide vocabulary is important to children's linguistic development.

Factors Affecting Language Development

There are many factors that affect the rate and manner in which children's language abilities develop. Some of these factors include:

- Developmental and medical issues
- Health of the home environment
- Socioeconomic status
- Socialization and exposure to a variety of texts, people, and experiences that provide new vocabulary

Building on Students' Current Language Skills

Because student backgrounds and skill levels are so diverse, it is essential for teachers to meet students where they are and build on their current language skills. They should identify current areas of strength to build on, while identifying and correcting areas of weakness. Instruction needs to be differentiated for the wide array of literacy skills that will be part of the classroom population.

Emergent Literacy Skills

Three foundational emergent literacy skills are the concept of print, the alphabetic principle, and letter-sound correspondence.

- The **concept of print** is the awareness that written letters have sounds and that they form words. Children should learn the structure of a book and have repeated exposure to text. This include how to hold a book, directionality, and the ability to track print as it's being read.

- The **alphabetic principle** is the understanding that words are made up of letters that have different sounds. This is developed through exposure to text and print.

- **Letter-sound correspondence** is the knowledge of the sounds that are associated with each letter of the alphabet.

Phonological and Phonemic Awareness

Phonological awareness is a broad skill that involves the understanding that language is made up of sound units (i.e. words, syllables, onsets, rhymes, etc.) and the ability to manipulate those units.

Phonemic awareness is a more specific skill that involves recognizing and manipulating phonemes, the smallest sound units within words.

Fundamental phonological awareness skills include the following:

- **Rhyming**- having an ending sound that corresponds with another (e.g. *cat, hat*)

- **Alliteration**- having the same beginning sound

- **Segmenting**- the ability to break a word up into its individual component sounds

- **Blending**- combining sounds to form words

Promoting Phonological Awareness Skills

Helping students understand phonemes and develop the ability to manipulate them is essential to their early literacy development. Some of the exercises with phonemes that are helpful for literacy development are:

- Using music, nursery rhymes, or other memorable jingles to introduce children to sounds, rhyming, and the rhythms and patterns of speech

- Phoneme isolation- recognizing separate phonemes in words

- Phoneme segmentation- separating a word into all of its phonemes

- Phoneme identification- finding common phonemes among different words

- Phoneme blending- giving a sequence of phonemes that create a word

- Phoneme addition- making a new word by adding a phoneme to an existing word

- Phoneme deletion- removing a phoneme from a word to make a new word

- Phoneme substitution- replacing a phoneme with another to form a new word

Word Recognition and Decoding

Decoding is the ability to apply the knowledge of letter-sound relationships in order to pronounce written words. Decoding requires several skills of its own. To successfully decode a word, a learner must be able to know the letters in the word and their appropriate sounds, remember each of these sounds in sequence, and put the sounds together to create a word.

Phonics is the understanding the sounds and printed letters are connected. Groups of sounds (with their associated letters) are organized into sequences to form words. Phonics provides a way for students to decode and encode words based on their component sounds.

Sight words are those short, familiar words which students come to recognize visually ("on sight") without having to decode the sounds.

Both phonics and sight words play an important role in literacy development. Sight words help children to get a jump-start on reading and to be able to tackle many small words that they will encounter frequently without having to spend the time and mental energy breaking them apart in order to decipher them. Phonics, meanwhile, gives students the skills they will need to tackle unfamiliar words and progress further in their literacy development with increasingly sophisticated words.

Phonics Patterns

Phonics follow certain predictable patterns. Within the system of phonics, there are letters or combinations of letters that make certain sounds. Words that contain these same sounds are said to contain the same phonics pattern. Teaching phonics patterns helps children with decoding by familiarizing them with common letter(s)-sound pairings. Some common phonics pattern types are:

- Long vowel sounds (the "a" in "ate," "rake," "shade")
- Short vowel sounds (the "i" in "hit," "tip," "crib")
- The long ("moon") and short ("good") "oo" sound
- Digraphs- two consonants or two vowels together that make a new sound (the "ph" in "photo" or the "au" is "cause")
- Consonant blends- combination consonant sounds (the "ft" in "gift")
- Hard and soft c and g sounds

Morphology

Morphology is the study of morphemes, which are the smallest units of sound that have meaning. These can include roots, prefixes, and suffixes. Students with a knowledge of morphemes and their meanings are better equipped to decode and decipher the meaning of new words. Instruction in morphemes gives students an important tool for the structural analysis of words.

Syllabication

A **syllable** is a unit of sound that contains one vowel sound. Onset and rime are subdivisions of syllables. **Onset** is the initial consonant sound of a syllable and **rime** is vowel sound plus the remainder of the syllable. For example, in the word "brick," "br" is the onset and "ick" is the rime.

Syllabication is the ability to correctly divide words into syllables. For developing readers and writers, syllabication helps to break words up into chunks that are easier to handle.

Encoding

Encoding is the ability to convert oral language into text. In order to encode, children must recognize the phonemes within words, know the letters that correspond with those sounds, and be able to put those into writing.

Stages of Writing Development

As children grow and develop, so do their writing skills. From their earliest scrawling eventually develops fully written compositions. Teachers should be familiar with how this process unfolds.

Stage	Description
Drawing	Expresses ideas through pictures; uses drawing as a form of communication
Scribbles	Uses scribbles as a form of writing; intends the scribbles to have meaning like writing
Letter-like Forms	Shapes start to look like letters but are not actual letters
Pre-communicative / Random letters	Writes actual letters but in patterns or strings that make no sense, uses letters without appropriate letter-sound correspondence
Invented spelling	Begins to form words but with own spelling; sometimes phonetic spelling; sometimes a single letter may stand for syllables or whole words; transitional spelling-improves over time
Conventional spelling	Spells correctly and resembles adult writing

Fluency is the ability to read text smoothly, without paying much conscious attention to the mechanics of reading. As learners' literacy skills develop, their fluency increases over time. Whereas beginning readers must decode and sound out many words, fluent readers give no thought to this and are able to read with speed and accuracy. Fluency plays an important role in reading comprehension. Once readers become more fluent and no longer have to spending their time and mental energy decoding words, they can focus more on comprehension.

The components of fluency are:

- **Rate**- the speed at which reading occurs

- **Accuracy**- a measure of the percentage of oral reading that is correct

- **Automaticity**-fast, accurate, effortless word recognition

- **Prosody**- the ability to read with appropriate intonation, expression, and rhythm

Calculating Fluency

Two common ways to express fluency numerically are **accuracy rate** and **words correct per minute (WCPM)**.

Accuracy rate (%)= (# of words correct / total # of words read) x 100

> Example: A student reads a 200-word passage and makes 8 errors. That makes the number of words correct 200 − 8 = 192.
>
> (192/200) x 100 = .96 x 100 = 96% accuracy

WCPM = (# of words correct/time in seconds) x 60 seconds

> Example: A student reads a 100-word passage in 2 minute and 10 seconds with 4 recorded errors. The number of words correct is 100 - 4 = 96. The time in seconds is 2(60) + 10 = 130 seconds.
>
> WCPM = (96/130) x 60 = 44.3 words per minute

Strategies for Improving Fluency

There are many strategies that can be used in the classroom to improve fluency among developing readers. These include:

- Readers' theater
- Practice with high-frequency words
- Repeated readings
- Oral reading
- Choral reading
- Echo reading
- Timed reading
- Poetry reading
- Paired reading

Writing and Research

Students must learn to write effectively in a variety of modes by utilizing the writing process and appropriate resource materials.

Topics Addressed:

1. The Writing Process
2. Types of Writing
3. Utilizing Resource Materials

As students learn to write, it is important for them to learn to write according to a clear process in order to ensure that their writing is given thought and quality. Throughout the writing process, peer editing can be a valuable tool to help students evaluate and revise their work.

The Five Stages of the Writing Process:

1. **Prewriting-** generate and record ideas for writing; this can include techniques such as brainstorming, semantic mapping, outlining, and using graphic organizers

2. **Rough Draft-** write down all of the ideas in an organized way

3. **Revise-** reread the rough draft and make changes to how the information is presented and organized; make sure tone, purpose, and audience are clear; add or delete content as needed

4. **Edit-** make changes to spelling, grammar, and other mechanics

5. **Publish-** create the final copy

Organization and Paragraphing

An important component of writing its organization. Writing should follow a clear and logical order, typically based either on chronology or to follow the progression of an argument.

Foundational to the organization of writing is paragraphing. Paragraphing helps to break long pieces of writing into chunks that are easier for the reader to take in. Each paragraph should contain a common theme. A new idea should prompt the beginning of a new paragraph.

A paragraph should contain a topic sentence, which introduces the idea of the paragraph. There should also be smooth and logical transitions between paragraphs (at the end of one paragraph and/or the beginning of the next) to help the reader to follow the progression of thought (see "Improving Writing Style" below for more on transitions).

Writing Style

Writing style includes such components as vocabulary, word choice, and fluidity. Students should be taught these elements of writing at increasing levels of sophistication as their literacy skills develop over their educational careers.

Some important elements include:

- **Precise language**- choosing words that are specific, and thus make a clearer mental picture for the reader (e.g., "poodle" instead of "dog")

- **Figurative language**- words or phrases that have meanings other than the literal meanings of the words, used for effect (e.g., simile, metaphor, hyperbole)

- **Transitions/linking words**- words or phrases used to move from one idea to the other; can include:

  - Location (e.g., on top of, above, below, across from)
  - Time (e.g., after, before, often)
  - Comparison (e.g., as, like, likewise, also)
  - Contrast (e.g., not, but, although, however)
  - Elaboration (e.g., also, again, additionally, furthermore)
  - Emphasis (e.g., all in all, as you can see, once again)
  - Conclusion (e.g., therefore, hence, in conclusion)

- **Temporal words**- words used to indicate time (e.g., at first, later, as soon as)

- **Sensory words**- words meant to appeal to the five senses, describing the look, sound, feel, taste, and smell of things (e.g., haggard, loud, fluffy, sweet, putrid)

- **Dialogue**- direct quotations spoken by characters in the writing; students must also be taught the proper punctuation for dialogue

- **Sentence variety**- Using different types of sentences structures makes writing more interesting for the reader.

Modes of Writing

There are six main modes of writing elementary students may encounter:

1. **Expositor/Informational Writing:** writing meant to instruct or explain

    Examples: research papers, reports, biographies

2. **Narrative Writing:** writing that tells a story

    Examples: novels, short stories, plays

3. **Persuasive Writing:** writing that expresses the author's point of view

    Examples: argumentative essay, editorial, reviews, advertisements

4. **Journaling/Letter Writing:** writing written as a personal message for a specific audience (either themselves or another person or organization)

    Examples: journals/diaries, learning logs, business letters, personal letters, emails

5. **Descriptive Writing:** writing meant to describe someone or something; uses language that appeals to the senses

    Examples: descriptive essays, character sketches

6. **Creative Writing:** writing drawn from the author's imagination

    Examples: fiction, poetry

Traits of Writing

All writing contains three main traits—tone, purpose, and audience. Keeping these in mind while writing and being intentional about the message you want to present is the best way to write effectively.

- **Tone-** the feeling or attitude that a piece of writing conveys

    Examples: humorous, sad, serious, uplifting

    Ensure that the tone is clear and appropriate for what you are trying to accomplish with the piece of writing.

- **Purpose-** why the author wrote the piece; what is the goal of this piece of writing?

    Examples: to persuade, to entertain, to inform, to instruct

    Keep this purpose in mind throughout to maintain focus of the goal of the writing. This will help to inform tone and language choices.

- **Audience-** who the piece is intended for; who is supposed to be reading this?

    Examples: children, adults, women, sports fans

    Ensure that the reading level and writing style are appropriate for that audience.

Organizational Structures of Writing

Writing can take on many forms and be organized in many ways. Structures of writing are devices that help the writing to accomplish its purpose. Some examples of writing structures are:

- **Description-** a writing mode for creating a mental picture of someone or something
- **Definition-** provides a statement of the exact meaning of something
- **Argument-** presents a case in favor of a particular point of view or opinion
- **Examples-** provide evidence to clarify an idea, add details, or to give support to an argument

The organization of a piece can help the writing to fulfill its purpose by conveying meaning in the most effective manner. Some common organizational structures of writing are:

Term	Definition
Descriptive	Provides a detailed description of someone or something
Comparison/Contrast	Examines the similarities and differences between two or more things
Cause and Effect	Presents causal relationships between a particular event or idea and those that follow it
Persuasive	Aims to convince the reader of a point of view; will include arguments and supporting evidence
Problem-Solution	Presents a problem, suggest and explains a possible solution, and discusses the potential effects of the solution
Sequential	Presents events in chronological order or presents a set of ordered steps; most common for a narrative

Evaluating and Incorporating Resources

There are many resources available to teachers and students in reading and language arts. In addition to traditional print materials, multimedia resources can be used to enhance literacy learning. Teachers should become familiar with the resources available in their schools and communities and integrate them into classroom learning. Additional, students should be familiarized with resource materials that they can use for research and to enhance their writing and presentations.

Sources of information fall under two major categories—primary and secondary sources.

- **Primary sources** are original sources that give a first-hand account of an event by someone who participated in it or observed it at the time that it was happening. Some examples of primary sources are diaries/journals, letters, interviews, and surveys.

- **Secondary sources** are created later by people who did not experience events first-hand. They draw on primary sources as their own source material and present their collected research to the reader. Some examples are research articles, books, and encyclopedias.

When evaluating sources, teachers and students should check for reliability, bias, accuracy, and up-to-date information.

Citing Sources

Students must be taught about plagiarism and the proper citing of sources in writing.

Plagiarism is passing off someone else's work as your own or using information from source materials without citing where they came from. Unintentional plagiarism can be prevented by teaching students the proper protocol for using ideas from source materials in their own work.

- Any information obtained from an outside source must be cited using proper formatting. The most common citation style in English Language Arts is MLA.

- Direct quotations from a source must be in quotation marks.

- Ideas taken from another source that are not in quotation marks should be a paraphrase into your own words.

Technology in the Classroom

There are many forms of technology available for use in Reading and Language Arts classroom. The use of technology can draw student interest, increase engagement, appeal to multiple learning styles, allow for differentiation, and help connect the content to students' daily lives.

Some common technology tools are:

- Computer presentation software for enhancing teacher-led instruction

- Interactive whiteboards

- Various forms of computer software

- Web Quests, where students utilize a predetermined list of websites to explore a topic

- Email to enhance communication for teachers, parents, students, and staff

- Wikis, where students contribute content to a webpage

- Video conferencing, which allows classes to connect in real-time with others around the world

- Podcasts, which are published audio recordings

Speaking, Listening, and Presenting

In addition to reading and writing, students must also learn to effectively communicate through speaking and listening.

Topics Addressed:

1. Promoting Listening Skills
2. Promoting Speaking and Presentation Skills

There are two types of listening-aesthetic listening and efferent listening. **Aesthetic listening** is listening for pleasure. **Efferent listening** is listening for the purpose of obtaining information from the speaker.

Listening skills are essential to literacy. Because so much early literacy is developed through oral communication, listening skills are an integral part of literacy development. Students must be able to listen carefully to a speaker, glean information aurally, and produce an appropriate response. It is therefore essential to promote listening skills in the classroom.

Listening is more than just hearing words. To listen, understand, and make meaning from spoken words requires active listening. There are several ways to be an effective listener:

- Focusing on the speaker

- Making eye contact

- Following directions

- Asking and responding to questions appropriately

- Paying attention to non-verbal communication

- Developing auditory memory

- Paraphrasing the speaker

- Visualizing what the speaker is saying

- Taking notes (possibly with a graphic organizer)

- Establish a purpose for listening at the beginning- what should you be listening *for*

Forms of Communication

There are two main types of communication—intrapersonal and interpersonal. Elementary-level students should be given instruction and support as they develop their skills in both of these areas.

Intrapersonal communication takes place within one single person, and includes that person's own thoughts and feelings. Some of the important elements of intrapersonal communication are:

- Self-concept: how a person views him or herself
- Attitude: feelings about a subject or situation
- Beliefs: what a person thinks to be true or false, good or bad, etc.
- Values: deeply rooted ideals, closely tied to beliefs
- Perception: how a person sees the world
- Goals and expectations: what a person wants or expects to happen
- Internal discourse: thought processes or imagined conversations
- Speaking to oneself aloud
- Writing to oneself (i.e. journaling)

Interpersonal communication is that which occurs between people. Interpersonal communication can include:

- Conversation
- Group discussion
- Written communication (email, letter, text, etc.)
- Public speaking
- Mass communication

In the classroom, collaborative conversations (discussions) are an important way for students to share with one another about their learning. Students should be encouraged to speak in groups with diverse members, as it is important for them to learn to communicate effectively with all types of people. It is also beneficial to bring a variety of perspectives into collaborative conversations. The classroom environment should be a comfortable, safe space where all feel free to participate in discussions about their learning and experiences.

Elements of Effective Presenting

When presenting, the speaker must take into consideration several aspects of the speaking process. Just like writing, speaking involves purpose, audience, and tone; however, since speaking is a live process rather than something that will be read later, and since the speaker will usually be visible to the audience, other special considerations must come into play. A speaker should make these considerations:

- **Purpose**- Why are you speaking? What do you hope to accomplish?

- **Tone**- What feeling should this have? Funny? Serious?

- **Audience**- Who are you speaking to? What are they like? What are their wants and needs? Should the speaking involve audience interaction (questioning, discussion)?

- **Occasion**- When and where is this taking place? Is what you are saying appropriate in this setting?

- **Format**- Is there an appropriate organizational format so that the audience can clearly follow the message?

- **Speaker**- How should you present yourself? What preparations should you make? Non-verbal communication is very important. Ensure that your body presents confidence and focus.

Grammar and Vocabulary

Teachers must be able to help students learn the standard conventions of the English language and to build their vocabularies.

Topics Addressed:

1. Conventions of the English Language
2. Vocabulary Development

The main components of written language are grammar, usage, and syntax. **Grammar** is the set of guidelines which govern the proper use of language. **Usage** refers to the proper use of words. **Syntax** is the manner in which words are arranged into sentences.

Parts of Speech

The basic types of words which make up the English language are known as parts of speech.

Part of Speech	Definition	Examples
Noun	Person, place, thing, or idea	boy, ball, Utah, democracy
Pronoun	Word that can take the place of a noun	he, it, something
Verb	Word that reflects an action or state of being	run, be
Adverb	A word that modifies a verb	quickly, very
Adjective	Descriptive word	happy, cold
Preposition	A word that indicates direction or position, or connects two ideas	on, off, above, to, of, from, at
Article	A word that comes before a noun that indicates whether the noun is specific or non-specific	a, an, the, this
Conjunction	A words that joins two words or phrases	for, and, nor, but, or, yet, so

Nouns

There are several different ways to classify nouns.

- Common vs. Proper

    - **Common noun**- general thing or idea; does not require capitalization.

      Examples: girl, country, religion

    - **Proper noun**- refers to a specific person, place, thing, or idea and DOES require capitalization.

      Examples: Alicia, Canada, Buddhism

- Singular vs. Plural

    - **Singular**- refers to only one thing. Examples: apple, goose

    - **Plural**- refers to more than one thing. Examples: apples, geese

- Subject vs. Object

    - The **subject** of a sentence is who or what the sentence is about. The subject performs the main verb of the sentence.

    - The **object** of a sentence is not the main subject of the sentence and has the verb *performed on it*.

      Example: *"Lisa enjoys listening to music."* In this sentence, "Lisa" is the subject and "music" is the object.

- Concrete vs. Abstract

    - **Concrete noun**- physical object. Examples: rock, building

    - **Abstract noun**- non-physical things, like ideas. Examples: creativity, sadness

Pronouns

Pronouns take the place of more specific nouns. The noun that a pronoun stands for is called the **antecedent.**

Example: *"Daniel works as a financial planner. He has worked at the same company for ten years."*

In this example, "he" is the pronoun and "Daniel" is the antecedent.

Just like nouns, pronouns can be classified as subjects or objects.

- Subject pronouns: he, she, I, we, they

- Object pronouns: him, her, me, us, them

Pronouns can also show possession.

- Examples: her, his, my, mine, ours, their

Verbs

There are three major types of verbs—action, linking, and helping.

- **Action verbs** show an action performed by the subject of a sentence.

   - Example: She <u>ran</u> to the store.

- **Linking verbs** connect the subject of the sentence to the additional information about the subject.

   - Example: The cat <u>was</u> black.

- **Helping verbs** are paired with another verb and are often used to indicate tense.

   - Example: School <u>will</u> be open tomorrow.

Verbs also indicate the time period in which the action is taking place. This is called **tense**. There are three major tenses—present, past, and future.

- **Present tense**- the action is occurring now

  Example: Anna lives in New York City.

- **Past tense**- the action occurred in the past

  Example: Anna lived in New York City.

- **Future tense**- the action will occur in the future

  Example: Anna will live in New York City.

Syntax

Syntax is the manner in which words are arranged into sentences. There are rules that govern proper syntax. A sentence must contain both a subject and a predicate.

- **Subject-** the part of the sentence that is *performing* the action; the noun that the sentence is about

  Example: Many trees and bushes grow in the forest.

- **Predicate-** gives information about the subject

  Example: Many trees and bushes grow in the forest.

A sentence *may* also contain one or more objects. As stated above, an object is a noun that receives the action of the verb. Objects can be direct or indirect.

- **Direct object-** directly receives the action of the predicate; answer the questions "whom?" or "what?"

- **Indirect object-** indirectly receives the action of the predicate; answer the questions "to whom/what?" "from whom/what?"

- Example: *"I gave a treat to the dog."*

  Subject- "I"

  Direct object- "treat"

  Indirect object- "dog"

Words are grouped together in several basic forms.

- **Phrases** are the most basic grouping of words. The words are related but may lack a subject (e.g. "went swimming) and/or a predicate (e.g. "my mother").

- **Clauses** are groups of words that contain both a subject and a verb. There are two types of clauses:
  - **Independent clause**- expresses a complete thought and could stand alone as a complete sentence
  - **Dependent clause**- does not express a complete thought and therefore could not stand alone as a complete sentence
  - Example: *"Because he got a flat tire, Tim was late to work."*

    "Tim was late to work" is an independent clause because it could stand alone as a complete sentence.

    "Because he got a flat tire" is a dependent clause because it could not stand alone as a complete sentence.

- **Sentences** are groups of words that contain both a subject and a predicate and express a complete thought.

Types of Sentences

A **sentence** is a grammatical structure that includes both a subject and a predicate and expresses a complete thought.

There are four main types of sentences:

1. **Declarative-** makes a statement and ends with a period.
   Example: My dog's name is Bruno.

2. **Imperative-** gives a command and usually ends with a period.
   Example: Give me that pencil.

3. **Interrogative-** asks a question and ends with a question mark.
   Example: Will you eat dinner with us tonight?

4. **Exclamatory-** shows strong feeling and ends with an exclamation point.
   Example: I'm so happy to see you!

Sentence Structure

There are four main types of sentence structures:

- **Simple sentences** contain one independent clause.
  Example: I went to the store.

- **Compound sentences** contain two or more independent clauses, joined by a conjunction or punctuation mark.
  Example: I went to the store and I bought eggs.

- **Complex sentences** contain one independent clause and at least one dependent clause.
  Example: On my way home from work, I went to the store.

- **Compound-complex sentences** contain at least two independent clauses and at least one dependent clause.
  Example: On my way home from work, I went to the store and I bought eggs, then I stopped for gas.

Vocabulary acquisition is an important part of literacy development. As readers mature, they should gain a more extensive vocabulary. There are several tools that can help students to interpret new vocabulary.

Affixes

Affixes are common beginnings (**prefixes**) and endings (**suffixes**) that add meaning to a base word. Understanding the meaning of an affix can help students make sense of the word.

Common Prefixes	Common Suffixes
A-	*-er*
Bi-	*-est*
Tri-	*-ing*
Un-	*-ly*
Pre-	*-fy*
Non-	*-it*
Dis-	*-is*
Anti-	*-tion*

Root Words

Root words are the most basic form of a word that conveys meaning. Many words in the English language have root words from other languages, such as Greek and Latin. There are hundreds of root words in the English language but a few examples are listed in the chart that follows.

Root Word	Meaning	Example
Aqua	Water	Aquatic
Demo	People	Democracy
Geo	Earth	Geography
Mal	Bad	Malice
Mono	One	Monologue
Poly	Many	Polytheism
Omni	All	Omniscient
Script	Write	Manuscript

Context Clues

Context clues are pieces of information in the text surrounding a new word that help provide meaning. Understanding the general meaning of a sentence or idea can help a reader to figure out the meaning of the unknown word.

Common types of context clues include:

- Synonyms- words that have the same meaning as the unknown word

- Antonyms- words that have the opposite meaning as the unknown word

- Explanations- words or phrases that explain the meaning of the unknown word

- Examples- words of phrases that provide examples of the unknown word

Multiple Exposures

An important part of learning new vocabulary is having multiple exposures to the new word, especially in different contexts. Seeing a word multiple types, used in a variety of ways, is the best way to cement a new word and its meaning in the memory.

Social Studies

Social Studies introduces students to topics in history, geography, government, civics, and economics in an effort to equip them to become informed and contributing members of a democratic society.

Test Structure

The Social Studies section makes up 25% of Subtest I. Social Studies, there are four major subcategories with which you must be familiar:

A. Information Processing Skills

B. Historical Understandings and Processes

C. Geography

D. Government, Civics, and Economics

Each subcategory is divided into topics, which state the skills you must be able to demonstrate on the exam.

Information Processing Skills

Students should be able to conduct social studies research and apply their findings to relevant situations and tasks.

Topics Addressed:

1. Social Studies Skills
2. Utilizing Resource Materials

Social studies is a field of inquiry in which students look into past or present society, looking for answers to a question about how the world works or why a situation is as it is. Students should be encouraged to ask critical questions and to investigate the answers. Social studies requires students to develop many different process skills. This can include:

- Questioning
- Gathering data
- Interpreting data from a variety of source types
- Evaluating sources
- Identifying cause and effect relationships
- Comparing and contrasting
- Drawing conclusions

There is a wide variety of source material available in Social Studies. The discipline requires students to become skilled at interpreting many types of texts, including books, articles, internet resources, maps, charts, graphs, political cartoons, and more.

Students should be able to recognize the differences between primary and secondary sources and to assess any type of source for credibility. They should learn to read historical texts with the author, purpose, original intended audience, and historical context in mind.

When reading historical interpretations, students should also keep in mind that historians, too, are the product of their own time periods and cultural backgrounds and that historical analyses can reflect bias. Students must learn to distinguish fact from opinion and keep the author's context and purpose in mind when using resources.

Social studies involves a high degree of reading, both primary and secondary sources. Students should understand the difference between primary and secondary sources and be able to analyze and utilize each appropriately.

Primary Sources

Primary sources are texts written by someone who was actually present during the time being studied. They provide a first-hand account of historical events as they lived through them. Primary sources can include letters, journals, newspaper articles, government documents, business ledgers, interviews, official records, speeches, pamphlets, or any other item created during the time period being studied.

 Because of the evolution of the English language over time and because of the varying levels of formality of language, primary sources can often be difficult texts for students to comprehend. Teachers should provide support such as vocabulary lists, scaffolding, and paraphrases where appropriate to help students understand difficult primary source texts.

When reading primary sources, students must also learn to be conscious of the context in which they were written and take into account factors such as the author's purpose, original intended audience, historical context, personal point of view, and bias.

Secondary Sources

Texts that are not primary sources are classified as **secondary sources**, meaning they were written after fact rather than by someone present in the time period being studied. Secondary sources may include textbooks, journal articles, biographies, or any other source written by an author who has researched, rather than lived through, a time period.

Even secondary sources are not necessarily objective, and students should still be conscious of the author's tone, purpose, audience, point of view, and bias when reading.

Historical Understandings and Processes

History encompasses the themes of time, continuity, and change. Students will study the history of the United States and specifically the state of Georgia.

Topics Addressed:

1. United States History
2. Georgia State History

The Pre-Colonial Era

Prior to the arrival of European explorers beginning in the fifteenth century, North America was inhabited by diverse indigenous populations. The North American landscape is diverse, including areas of plains, desert, and mountains, and those different environments resulted in vastly different Native American cultural groups across the continent.

Depending on their environment, some tribes used agriculture, growing important crops such as maize (corn), potatoes, and squash, while others relied on hunting and gathering. Tribes living in coastal areas relied more heavily on fishing.

Native American groups typically had traditional economies based on bartering. Instead of using money, goods would be exchanged directly for other goods. Trade between tribes was common as a way to obtain needed supplies.

There are numerous indigenous groups that existed (many of whom still exist, albeit usually relocated) throughout North America. Two major groups were the Iroquois and the Pueblo.

The Iroquois were not a single tribe, but rather an organized confederation of five original nations—Cayuga, Onondaga, Seneca, Oneida, and Mohawk. The Tuscarora joined the confederacy later. Today, the Iroquois are known as the Six Nations. The Iroquois originated in the American Northeast, largely in what is now New York. They are noted for their organized government and the cooperation among their nations.

The Pueblo lived in the American Southwest. The Pueblo elected a chief (rather than it being a strictly hereditary office, as was common elsewhere), making them one of the earliest representative governments in the world. The Pueblo are also noted for the way in which they adapted to their environment by creating houses and other buildings both from adobe mud-bricks and in the faces of cliffs.

European Exploration

Starting in the 1400s, European powers began to look to expand their influence outward. They sent explorers to find new trade routes and new lands that could be used for their natural resources. During this period, European explorers learned about the existence of the North and South American continents and began to colonize these areas, which were collectively called the New World. Part of this territory would one day become the United States.

The three main motivations for exploration of the New World were:

- Glory- the desire for personal status and to bring prestige to the home country

- God- convert native populations to Christianity

- Gold- get riches for themselves and natural resources, new trade routes, and trading partners for the home country

Students should be familiar with some of the major explorers who navigated the Americas.

Explorer	Nation	Achievements
John Cabot	Britain	Explored the east coast of Canada
Christopher Columbus	Italy, sailed for Spain	"Discovered" North America while looking for a western route to India
Amerigo Vespucci	Italy	The first to realize the Americas were not part of Asia; America is named after him
Vasco de Balboa	Spain	First to reach the Pacific by crossing Central America
Juan Ponce de Leon	Spain	First to explore Florida while searching for the Fountain of Youth
Ferdinand Magellan	Spain	First to circumnavigate the globe by sailing around the southern tip of South America
Hernan Cortez	Spain	Conquered Mexico from the Aztecs
Francisco Pizarro	Spain	Conquered the Incan Empire
Jacques Cartier	France	Explored Canada and claimed it for France
Fernando de Soto	Spain	Discovered the Mississippi River
Francisco Coronado	Spain	Explored the American southwest
Walter Raleigh	Britain	Established English colonies in North America
Henry Hudson	Britain	Explored northeastern North America and the Arctic
James Cook	Britain	Explored the Pacific; discovered Hawaii

From Colonies to a New Nation

The British established thirteen colonies along the east coast of what is now the United States. Within the Thirteen Colonies, there were three main regions—New England, Middle Atlantic, and the Southern Colonies. Each area developed its own unique characteristics.

Region	Colonies	Characteristics
New England Colonies	New Hampshire, Massachusetts, Rhode Island, Connecticut	• Rocky soil was poor for farming • Relied on fishing and shipping industries • Most people lived in or near towns • Major city: Boston
Middle Atlantic Colonies	New York, New Jersey, Pennsylvania, Delaware	• Good conditions for farming • The "breadbasket" of the colonies • Fur trade • Major city: Philadelphia
Southern Colonies	Maryland, Virginia, North Carolina, South Carolina, Georgia	• Plantation farming (tobacco, indigo, rice, cotton) • Slavery • More rural population • Major cities: Richmond, Charleston

The Thirteen Colonies eventually wanted to rule themselves rather than continue to be controlled by Great Britain. This resulted in the American Revolution.

After the American Revolution, these colonies would become the first thirteen states. They served as the foundation for a nation that would eventually grow to include fifty states across a vast expanse of territory.

Causes of the American Revolution

When the colonies were first settled, they relied heavily on help from the British. They needed British supplies, British money, the British government to keep order, and the British military for protection. Over time, as the colonies grew more established and stronger, they became more self-sufficient. They no longer relied on the British for everything. They even made their own local governments to make decisions. The less they depended on the British, the more they felt like they didn't need them anymore and that they could govern themselves.

In the late 1700s, the British found themselves in need of money after the costly French and Indian War, so they began to impose many new taxes on the colonists. These included:

- Stamp Act (1765)

- Townshend Acts (1767)

- Tea Act (1773)

- Intolerable Acts (1774)

The colonists did not have representation in the British Parliament, which levied the taxes, so they didn't think it was fair that they should be taxed. After failed attempts at negotiation and compromise, tensions escalated and eventually erupted into war—the American Revolution.

Boston, Massachusetts played an important role in the events leading up to the American Revolution. The **Boston Massacre** (1770) in which British soldiers killed five colonial protestors further inflamed colonists against the British. The **Boston Tea Party** (1773) occurred when colonists protested the aforementioned taxes by boarding a ship and dumping tea into Boston Harbor. The Intolerable Acts were largely a response to the Boston Tea Party and included provisions designed to punish Boston specifically, including the closing of Boston Harbor.

Major Events in the American Revolution

The **American Revolution** began in Massachusetts with the **Battle of Lexington and Concord** in 1775. This was soon followed by the **Battle of Bunker Hill**.

The next summer, representatives from the colonies signed a document called the **Declaration of Independence**, which listed the reasons for the rebellion and stated that the United States was to be an independent country. It was signed on July 4, 1776.

Britain was not ready to accept American independence, however, and the war continued. While the British army was more established, better trained, and had larger numbers, the Americans had the advantage of fighting on their own familiar territory and eventually secured aid from the French. The Americans won the war with a final victory at the **Battle of Yorktown** in 1781. The war officially concluded with the signing of the Treaty of Paris in 1783.

Forming a New Nation

The new nation had to create a government for itself. The first system they tried was organized around a document called the **Articles of Confederation**. This made the new government too weak, however, and it ultimately failed.

In 1787, the Articles of Confederation were replaced with a new form of government, outlined in the **U.S. Constitution**. The Constitution set up a federal system with a three-branch national government. Revolutionary War hero George Washington was chosen as the first President of the United States.

U.S. Expansion

Over the course of its history, the United States made several major expansions, enlarging its land from thirteen original states to the current fifty.

The British had holdings in North America other than the Thirteen Colonies. Part of this was in Canada, and remained in British hands following the American Revolution. Some of this territory was adjacent to the Thirteen Colonies and became a part of the new United States. Originally, the Thirteen Colonies turned into the first thirteen states of the United States. The additional territory, which included lands between the Appalachian Mountains and the Mississippi River, was eventually settled. The territories each eventually applied for statehood and became Ohio, Indiana, Illinois, Alabama, Mississippi, Michigan, and Wisconsin.

The next major territorial expansion of the United States occurred in 1803 when President Thomas Jefferson bought the Louisiana Territory from France. The **Louisiana Purchase** doubled the size of the nation, adding what would eventually become Louisiana, Arkansas, Missouri, Iowa, Minnesota, North Dakota, South Dakota, Kansas, Nebraska, Oklahoma, Colorado, Wyoming, and Montana.

This major expansion gave birth to the idea that the United States should one day possess the lands all the way to the Pacific Ocean. The belief that this was the nation's God-given right became known as **Manifest Destiny**. Fueled by this spirit, the nation continued to expand.

The United States purchased Florida from Spain in 1819. In 1845, it annexed Texas, which was at the time an independent republic. The Oregon Territory was acquired in 1846. The **Mexican Cession** of 1848, which followed the Mexican-American War, resulted in the acquisition of the territories that would become California, Nevada, New Mexico, Arizona, and Utah. The **Gadsden Purchase** (1853, from Mexico) completed the territories of Arizona and New Mexico. Alaska was purchased from Russia in 1867 and Hawaii was annexed in 1898.

Civil War and Reconstruction

The young nation soon became divided over the issue of slavery. States in the South permitted slavery while those in the North did not. The interests of the two regions were relatively balanced in Congress until new states started to be added in the western territories. Pro- and anti-slavery supporters each feared losing power in Congress and fought for the new states to join their side.

Eventually, the conflict escalated and the South seceded (left) the Union, forming the Confederate States of America. The United States, led by President Abraham Lincoln, did not accept the secession and fought the **Civil War** (1861-1865) in order to preserve the unity of the nation. In the end, the North won, the nation was reunited, and slavery was abolished with the passage of the **13th Amendment**.

The period following the Civil War was known as **Reconstruction**. During this period, the government worked to rebuild the South, which had been devastated by the war. Methods used during Reconstruction were controversial and led to continued resentment by many southerners. Following Reconstruction, African Americans, now free from slavery, found themselves subject to legal discrimination in the South, including segregation and voting restrictions. Many migrated to cities in the North.

Industrialization

In the mid-1800s, the United States became part of an international phenomenon known as the Industrial Revolution. During this period, rapid advancements were made in technology that allowed for production to change over from cottage industries to factory systems. This allowed for mass-production of goods.

The impact of the Industrial Revolution was far-reaching. Goods could now be manufactured quickly and cheaply. This led to great economic growth for the United States. Factories provided new jobs for many people, including the nation's large influx of immigrants, many of whom were drawn to the United States during this period because of the political freedoms and economic opportunities the country had to offer. All of those factory jobs also drew people into cities, leading to widespread urbanization. It also led to the homogenization of culture as people across the nation were able to access and afford the same goods. Technologies produced during the Industrial Revolution would shape the modern world.

Some negative effects of the Industrial Revolution included hazardous working conditions in factories, poor living conditions in crowded urban areas, and pollution. The Progressive Movement of the early 20th century, led by President Teddy Roosevelt, sought to put in place regulations to help solve some of these problems, including anti-monopoly laws, new economic rules and environmental regulations.

World Wars I and II

World War I

Though it initially sought neutrality, the United States became involved in World War I (1914-1918) in 1917 due to a combination of factors, including the Germans' use of unrestricted submarine warfare, the sinking of the *Lusitania*, and the Zimmerman Telegram.

The United States joined on the side of the Allied Powers and helped lead them to victory. The war ended with the Treaty of Versailles.

The Interwar Period

Following World War I, the United States once again sought isolation from the rest of the world, not wanting to be dragged into another war. For this reason, it declined to join the newly formed League of Nations.

The 1920s saw a period of economic prosperity for the United States. The decade became known as the **Roaring Twenties**. Economically, it was marked by mass consumerism, buying on credit, and the growth of the power of the stock market.

Socially, this was the period when women gained the right to vote, when the automobile became popular, and when jazz music came to be.

The high period of the 1920s came to an abrupt end in 1929, when a massive stock market crash led to the **Great Depression**. A combination of factors, including excess spending, speculation, agricultural overproduction, and buying on margin led to the economic downturn. During the Great Depression, inflation and unemployment were high, banks failed, and families throughout the nation found themselves enduring economic hardship.

President Franklin D. Roosevelt alleviated some of the suffering in the Great Depression with his **New Deal** programs, which gave the government a more active role in the economy. The Great Depression did not come to an end, however, until World War II jumpstarted the economy by providing industrial jobs and demanding a high output of military goods.

World War II

When **World War II** (1939-1945) broke out in Europe, the United States tried to remain neutral. Once again, however, it was eventually pulled into the conflict. The immediate cause of the U.S. entry into World War II was the Japanese bombing of **Pearl Harbor** in 1941.

The United States joined the war on the side of the Allies and fought both in Europe against the Germans and Italians and in Asia against the Japanese. U.S. forces were able to provide necessary reinforcement to Allied troops in Europe, securing the victory on that front. After a drawn out battle in the Pacific, the United States brought the war to a swift end with the dropping of the first **atomic bombs** on the Japanese cities of Hiroshima and Nagasaki.

The war concluded with the Treaty of Paris. The **United Nations** was soon established as an international peacekeeping organization to replace the League of Nations. The United States joined as a prominent member.

The Post-World War II Era

The Cold War

Following World War II, Europe was devastated by the conflict, leaving two superpowers left on the world stage—the United States and the Soviet Union. The two nations had competing ideologies (capitalism vs. communism; individualism vs.

collectivism) and both wished to spread their ideals to other nations. This led to rivalry. The conflict was greatly intensified by the fact that both sides had nuclear weapons. An attack by either would have had devastating global consequences, so the **Cold War** became decades of competition and threats without direct military conflict.

The two sides fought indirectly in two major **proxy wars**, in which each nation backed a side in a foreign civil war. The **Korean War** (1950-1953) saw communist North Korea, aided by the U.S.S.R., fight to take over South Korea, aided by the United States. The conflict ended in a ceasefire with no changes in boundaries. The **Vietnam War** (1956-1975) saw communist North Vietnam (along with communists in South Vietnam called the Viet Cong), aided by the U.S.S.R., attempt to take over South Vietnam, backed by the United States. The United States eventually withdrew from the long and unpopular war, and the North won, uniting the two territories into the single communist nation of Vietnam. The Cold War came to an end in 1991 when the Soviet Union dissolved due to internal problems.

The Post-Cold War Era

The 1990s were marked by an period of economic growth and prosperity. The decade also saw the rise of the Internet Age, which has revolutionized modern society. The United States was involved in international conflicts during the 1990s, including the Persian Gulf War and Bosnia.

The early twenty-first century has been marked domestically by an economic downturn. In foreign policy, the War on Terror (in response to terrorist attacks on September 11, 2001) has shaped more than a decade of international relations. The United States has fought in long wars in Afghanistan and in Iraq.

20th Century Developments and Transformations

Social Changes

Many important social changes occurred during the twentieth century. Two of the most significant of these were increased rights for women and for African-Americans.

The women's rights movement saw its first major national success in 1920 with the passage of the 19th Amendment, which granted women the right to vote. Another major push for women's rights occurred in the 1970s, when the National Organization led the fight for equal rights for women in all areas. This included the

Equal Rights Amendment (ERA) which was passed by Congress but failed to get approval by enough states to be added to the Constitution.

African-Americans, too, fought for their rights throughout much of the twentieth century. In the time since the Civil War, African-Americans faced discrimination, violence, segregation, disenfranchisement, and unequal opportunities. The Civil Rights Movement, which really gained momentum in the 1960s, sought to change that. Some of the key leaders in the Civil Rights Movement included Martin Luther King, Jr., Malcolm X, and Rosa Parks.

Some of the major developments in the Civil Rights Movement were:

- *Brown v. Board of Education of Topeka, Kansas* (1954) desegregated public schools, saying that the principle of "separate but equal" established in the earlier case of *Plessy v. Ferguson* (1896) led to facilities and conditions that were "inherently unequal."

- The Civil Rights Act (1964) outlawed discrimination based on race.

- The Voting Rights Act (1965) outlawed literacy tests and poll taxes as voting requirements, which had previously been used in some states to keep African-Americans from voting.

Technological Advancements

Technological advancements were rapid and far-reaching in the twentieth century. The wide array of innovations has changed modern society. Below is just a small sampling of the many developments of the twentieth century that have had a lasting impact.

- Communication technology- radio, television, cellular phones, computers, the internet

- Transportation technology- automobile, airplane, space travel

- Weaponry- nuclear weapons, chemical weapons

Prior to the arrival of European colonists, the land that is now Georgia was inhabited by Native American tribes, including the Cherokee, Creek, and Yamasee. The area was explored by the Spanish, the French, and the English, who then fought one another for dominance. Eventually, England took control of the territory.

The English began forming permanent settlements in Georgia beginning in the 1730s. The first colonists were led by James Oglethorpe, considered the founder of Georgia. Following the American Revolution, Georgia became one of the 13 original states in the newly formed United States of America. It was the fourth state to ratify the U.S. Constitution in 1788.

Georgia's population continued to grow, aided by the discovery of gold in the mountains, which drew settlers. As the state's white population grew, they began to pressure the government to expel the Cherokee, who continued to hold onto their ancestral lands. They were expelled by the U.S. government under President Andrew Jackson's 1830 Indian Removal act. The Cherokee were relocated to reservations west of the Mississippi along a route that became known as the Trail of Tears.

Prior to the Civil War, Georgia, like much of the Deep South, was a slave state with a thriving cotton industry. Georgia seceded from the Union in February of 1861, joining the Confederate States of America. During the Civil War, Georgia became the site of important campaigns, including General Sherman's March to the Sea. At the conclusion of the Civil War, with the Confederate loss, Georgia rejoined the Union. Following the war, the state worked to rebuild during the period of Reconstruction.

In the following decades, Florida underwent industrialization, warfare, rights movements and cycles of economic booms and recessions along with the rest of the nation.

Geography

Geography is the study of the physical features of the Earth. This includes both the natural landscape and the ways that humans interact with it.

Topics Addressed:

1. Elements of Geography
2. The World in Spatial Terms
3. Places and Regions
4. Physical Systems
5. Human Systems
6. Environment and Society
7. Uses of Geography

The study of geography is organized into six essential elements:

1. The World in Spatial Terms

- The geographic organization of the world

2. Places and Regions

- Place refers to an area whose boundaries are manmade, as well the physical and human characteristics of the location.
- Regions are geographic areas with unifying physical and/or human characteristics.

3. Physical Systems

- The natural landscape and processes of the Earth

4. Human Systems

- Processes and man-made societal structures by which humans organized themselves

5. Environment and Society

- The way that humans relate to their geographic surroundings

6. Uses of Geography

- How to study geography and the ways in which geographic knowledge can be utilized

Spatial categories are used to divide the world into parts with common characteristics in order to better understand it.

The Earth is divided in halves called **hemispheres**. The Northern and Southern Hemispheres are divided by a line of latitude called the **equator**. The Eastern and Western Hemispheres are divided by a line of longitude called the **prime meridian**.

The largest masses on Earth are its seven **continents**—North America, South America, Europe, Asia, Africa, Australia, and Antarctica.

The largest bodies of water are called **oceans**. The world's oceans are the Atlantic, the Pacific, the Indian, the Arctic, and the Southern Oceans.

Specific places on Earth are identified as locations. A **location** is where a place is in the world, physically. Location can be absolute or relative.

- **Absolute location**- precise location on a map, given by coordinates (e.g. New York City is located at 40.7127° N, 74.0059° W.)

- **Relative location- the location of a place with respect to other places (e.g. New York City** is northwest of Philadelphia.)

Places are areas whose boundaries are man-made. These include countries, states, territories, counties, cities, towns, etc.

Regions are areas that have common characteristics, both in the physical makeup of the land and in the culture of the people who live there. On the worldwide stage, some commonly identified regions include Latin America, the Middle East, and Southeast Asia.

Regional Geography of the United States

Within the United States, the major regions are the West, the Southwest, the Midwest, the South, the Mid-Atlantic, and New England.

- The West includes the Pacific coastal area, which results in a temperate, wet climate. Running through this region are the Rocky Mountains, the largest mountain range in North America.

- The Southwest has a more hot, dry climate. Culturally, it is heavily influenced by the neighboring nation of Mexico.

- The Midwest contains America's Great Plains, which conduct a large share of the nation's agricultural production. The Mississippi River flows through the eastern portion of the region and the Great Lakes and Canada border it in the north.

- The South has a warmer, more humid climate, as much of it borders the Atlantic Ocean and the Gulf of Mexico. The Appalachian Mountains run along the eastern portion and the Mississippi Delta is located in Louisiana.

- The Mid-Atlantic region borders the Atlantic Ocean and the Great Lakes. It is home to mountains including the Adirondacks and the Catskills.

- New England is located along the rocky northeastern Atlantic coast of the United States.

Regional Geography of Georgia

Georgia is located in the Southeastern United States, along the Atlantic coast. Its capital is Atlanta. Georgia's climate is primarily humid subtropical, with hot, wet summers and mild winters.

Georgia's geography is distinguished by several regions:

- The Appalachian Mountains, including the Ridge and Valley area, are located in the northwest corner of the state. The mountains are the site of mining, and some farming is conducted in the valleys.

- The Blue Ridge Mountains are located in northeastern Georgia. Historically, the area was the site of a lot of mining activity. Today, while there is still some mining in the area, the Blue Ridge Mountains tend to be primarily a recreational area. The state's highest point— Brasstown Bald—is located there. The Chattahoochee River—Georgia's longest—begins in the Blue Ridge Mountains.

- The central plateau region of the state is known as the Piedmont. This area is the most highly industrialized in the state and is home to most of Georgia's major cities.

- The Atlantic Coastal Plain stretches across the southern part of the state. Agriculture is the dominant economic activity in the Upper Coastal Plain, while the Lower Coastal Plain along the Atlantic is the site of shipping and recreational activity.

- Georgia also includes thirteen islands off its Atlantic Coast. These include the Golden Isles.

Physical systems are the component of geography concerned with the natural landscape and processes of the Earth.

Geographic Terms

Students will need to know important geographic terms used to describe the Earth's characteristics.

Term	Definition	Example in the U.S.	Example Outside the U.S.
Archipelago	Chain of islands	Hawaii	Japan
Bay	A body of water that is an inlet to a larger body of water such as an ocean or a sea	San Francisco Bay	Bay of Bengal
Canal	A man-made waterway	Erie Canal	Panama Canal
Channel	A narrow body of water that connects two other bodies of water	Houston Ship Channel	English Channel
Delta	Low, wet, triangular piece of land at the mouth of a river	Mississippi Delta	Nile Delta
Desert	Area with little to no precipitation	Desert	Sahara Desert
Gulf	A large body of water partially enclosed by land that connects to an ocean or sea	Gulf of Mexico	Persian Gulf
Island	A piece of land surrounded on all sides by water	Puerto Rico	Cuba
Isthmus	A very narrow strip of land connecting two larger pieces of land with water on both sides	Madison Isthmus	Isthmus of Panama
Lake	A body of water completely surrounded by land	Lake Ontario	Lake Titicaca
Mountain	A very high rocky formation	Rocky Mountains	Andes Mountains

Term	Definition	Example in the U.S.	Example Outside the U.S.
Peninsula	A piece of land with water on three sides	Florida	India
Plains	Flat, grassy lands	The Great Plains	The Great Steppe
River	A long, flowing body of water that empties into a larger body of water	The Mississippi River	The Amazon River
Sea	A large saltwater body, smaller than an ocean	Bering Sea	Mediterranean Sea
Valley	Low area between mountains	Death Valley	Danube Valley

Climates and Biomes

Climates are long-term weather patterns for a particular area. The primary climates on Earth are:

- **Tropical**- hot and wet year-round

- **Dry**- temperature varies widely from day to night; very little precipitation

- **Temperate**- warm and wet in the summer, cool and dry in the winter

- **Continental**- found on large land masses, this climate has fairly low precipitation and temperatures can vary widely

- **Polar**- very cold; permanently frozen ground

Biomes are large areas that have distinct sets of plant and animal life that are well-adapted to the environment. Biomes are classified according to geography and climate. The major biomes are:

- **Alpine**- mountain regions that are cold and snowy

- **Chaparral**- hot and dry; landscape varies- could contain plains, hills, and/or mountains

- **Deciduous forest-** contains many trees; four distinct seasons (spring, summer, fall, winter)

- **Desert-** flat land with very little precipitation

- **Grasslands-** interior flatlands with lots of grass and other low plant life; tropical or temperate climate

- **Rainforest-** tropical climate; dense vegetation

- **Savanna-** grasslands with warm temperatures year-round with a dry and a rainy season

- **Taiga-** cold, snowy winters and warm, humid summers

- **Tundra-** very cold; little vegetation; polar climate

Humans systems are processes and man-made societal structures by which humans organized themselves.

The Organization of Human Societies

Throughout history, humans have organized themselves into societies for their mutual benefit. Societal living offers protection and the ability to pool resources. In order to maintain order in societies, people tend to organize in certain ways. Societal structures range from the very simple to the complex.

- **Family**- The most basic organizational structure of societies is the family unit. Family structures and relationships vary across cultures. Some societies are patriarchal (led by the eldest male) while others are matriarchal (led by the eldest female). Some cultures value filial piety (respect for elders) more than others. Culture also dictates traditions for marriage and raising children.

- **Neighborhoods and Communities**- Groups of families living together in close proximity create neighborhoods and communities. Culture impacts the way that communities cooperate or compete. Some cultures place a high value on self-sufficiency, while others see more merit in interdependence.

- **Formal political structures**- Some structures of society are formal and political in nature. Geographical boundaries and governments dictate who is part of a group. These organizational structures range from villages and towns at the local level up to very large scale organizations like nations and empires.

- **Informal cultural structures**- People can belong to more informal organizations as well. This can include ethnic or cultural groups, religions and religious organizations, and other socially-based groups.

Population Growth

The world population is growing, but the rate of growth has varied greatly over time. Birth and death rates, which cause populations to grow or decline, are influenced by many factors, including:

- Supplies of food, water, and other resources
- Violence
- Disease
- Medical advancements
- Technology

Patterns of Migration

The movement of groups of people is called migration. Migration takes two major forms:

1. Immigration- movement into a new area or country
2. Emigration- movement out of an area or country

Migration is caused by many factors. Factors that cause people to emigrate from their homeland are called "push factors." Factors that draw people to immigrate to a new area are called "pull factors." Here are some common ones:

Push Factors	Pull Factors
Warfare	Peace
Disease	Health
Famine	Resources
Lack of opportunity	Economic opportunities such as jobs
Economic struggle	Opportunity for social mobility
Lack of social mobility	

Cultural Transmission

Throughout learning about social studies, students will encounter information about people groups, both past and present, with varied cultural backgrounds. Students should try to gain understanding of how peoples' cultural backgrounds are tied to their interactions with the world around them.

Cultures undergo change over time, and a major reason for this is that cultures frequently come into contact with one another and ideas are shared. This is called the **transmission of culture** or **cultural diffusion**.

Culture is transmitted by many means, including:

- Trade and commerce
- Travel/exploration
- Warfare and conquest
- Missionary activities
- International cooperation
- Communication via technology

Human Effects on the Environment

Humans, more than any other creatures, have the capacity to alter their environments. Human settlements have an enormous impact on the physical systems of the Earth. One major way that humans affect the natural environment is through construction. Building transportation systems, buildings, and other structures alters the landscape and displaces the organisms that once inhabited that space.

Another way humans affect the environment is by using natural resources. Earth has a limited amount of natural resources and growing human populations and advanced technology have increased the demand for those resources over time, putting a strain on the natural environment. Along with construction and the use of natural resources also comes pollution. Human activity creates waste byproducts that can be harmful to the environment.

Environmental Effects on Humans

Likewise, physical systems affects humans and they must learn to adapt to environmental factors. Physical features influence where humans will settle, what kind of communities and industries they can build there, and how easily those communities will be able to connect with other communities. For example, because of the difficult terrain, fewer people live in mountainous regions than in lowlands. Those societies that do live in the mountains have made adaptations such as terrace farming in order to survive in that environment. These communities have historically also found themselves isolated from the outside world due to the natural barriers that the mountains create. Geography also affects day to day life in ways such as the foods that people eat, the clothing they wear, and the type of housing they live in.

The study of geography has many uses. It helps to make sense of the world and to picture the physical relationships between people, groups and environments. Historically, it helps people understand why societies have settled where they have and why they developed in the ways that they did. It helps to understand the causes of conflicts between both historical and contemporary groups. It can also help to plan for the future by allowing for the examination of the distribution of people and resources throughout the world.

Using Visual Tools

There are many visual tools that can aid students in understanding Social Science content. These include maps, charts, political cartoons, photographs, illustrations, multimedia sources, and more. Students should analyze these sources carefully, checking for labels, captions, scales, and other details that can help them understand the information in the source.

Maps

One particularly important skill in Social Studies is knowing how to read and create maps. A **map** is a visual representation of a physical space. There are many types of maps, including physical maps, political maps, topographic maps, thematic maps, climate maps, historical maps, and population maps. Some key features of maps that students should know are:

- **Lines of latitude and longitude**- lines marking the distance of a location from the equator (latitude) and the prime meridian (longitude)

- **Compass rose**- symbol on a map showing the cardinal directions

- **Legend/Key**- box on a map that shows what the symbols and/or colors on a map represent

- **Scale**- Shows how distances on the map compare to real-life distances

Government, Civics, and Economics

Students study the government in order to better understand the society in which they live and so that they may become informed, active citizens of the democracy. It is important for students to understand how the government operates, as well as the rights and responsibilities of the nation's citizens.

Economics is a social science concerned with how goods and services are produced, bought, and sold. Students should understand the fundamental economic principles, basic components of economic systems, and the relationship between economics and society.

Topics Addressed:

1. The Purposes, Structures, and Functions of Government

2. The Government of the United States

3. Principle of Democratic Citizenship

4. Economic Systems

5. Resources, Scarcity, Choice, and Competition

Governments are created to maintain order in a society and for the protection of individuals' lives, liberties, and properties. Governments establish laws in order to protect these things and to prevent conflicts among people.

Functions of Government

Regardless of the type of government, there are several functions that a government is expected to carry out. The type of government will influence how to and what extent these are enacted.

The basic functions of government are:

- Establishing laws
- Public safety
- Maintaining order
- Providing public services
- Defense
- Economic activity
- Education

Structures of Government

In order to carry out these functions, governments consist of some form and combination of the following basic structures:

- Legislature- makes the laws
- Court system- provides justice and settles disputes
- Executive-enforces the laws
- Bureaucracy- carries out the day-to-day functions of the government

The United States is considered a democratic republic. The operations of its government are outlined in the **United States Constitution**.

The basic constitutional principles include:

- **Popular sovereignty**- the right of the people to rule through voting

- **Limited government**- the government can only do the duties assigned to it by the Constitution and members of the government are not above the law

- **Federalism**- the division of power between national and state governments

- **Separation of powers**- the division of power between three branches of government

- **Checks and balances**- the ability of each branch to limit the power of the other branches

- **Flexibility**- the ability of the Constitution to adapt with the times as necessary

The Federal System

The government of the United States is a **federal system**, which means that power is divided between the national and state governments. Powers allocated to the national government (e.g. the military, warfare, interstate commerce, coining money) are called **delegated powers**. Powers that belong to the states (e.g. professional licensing, intrastate commerce, establishing schools) are called **reserved powers**. Powers that are shared by both the national and state governments (e.g. taxation, making laws, having courts) are called **concurrent powers**. Within each state, there are also local governments that make day-to-day decisions affecting their communities.

Branches of Government

At the national level, power is divided between three branches of government. This **separation of powers** ensures that no one person or group has all the power. The branches are the executive, legislative, and judicial branches. Each branch has its own responsibilities, which include **checks and balances** on the other branches.

	Executive Branch	Legislative Branch	Judicial Branch
Who?	President, Vice-President	Congress (House of Representatives and Senate)	Supreme Court
How Chosen	Elected for 4-year terms (maximum of 2 terms)	House: elected for 2-year terms Senate: elected for 6-year terms	Appointed by the President and approved by Congress; serve for life
Main Duty	Enforce the laws	Make the laws	Interpret the laws
Checks on Other Branches	• Appoints Supreme Court nominees • Can veto laws	• Must approve Supreme Court nominees • Can override presidential veto • Can impeach president or Supreme Court justices	• Can declare laws or presidential actions unconstitutional

The Electoral System

Citizens aged 18 and older are eligible to vote and must register to do so in their local district. Elections in the United States are held on the first Tuesday in November. Presidential elections are held every four years and congressional elections are held every two years. The frequency of elections for state and local officials may vary by state.

Though it is not in the Constitution, the United States has, through practice, developed into a two-party system. While there have been other major parties in the past, currently, the two major parties are the Democratic Party and the Republican Party. While other parties are allowed to run candidates, they rarely gain the support needed to win seats, especially at the national level.

For many offices, the major parties hold **primary elections** (typically in the spring preceding the general election) in which voters choose who among a pool of candidates will become the official candidate for the party. The winning candidates from each party then face off against one another in the **general election** in November. The candidate with the most votes wins the seat.

In the case of presidential elections, a special electoral body known as the **electoral college** plays an important role in the election. Following the count of the popular vote in the general election, the vote then moves to the electoral college. The electoral college is made up of representatives from each state. Each state receive a certain number of electoral votes based on its population. The candidate with the most popular votes in each state receives that state's electoral votes. The electoral votes are then tallied and it is those votes that decide the election. Typically, the nationwide popular vote and the electoral vote result in the election of the same candidate, but on rare occasions, a candidate may win the presidency without having won the popular vote by having enough electoral votes.

Amendments to the Constitution

The Constitution was intended to be flexible, allowing it to change as necessary with the times. This is why it includes a process for adding **amendments**, or changes, to the document. Currently, there are twenty-seven amendments. The first ten amendments are collectively known as the **Bill of Rights** and they outline citizens' basic rights and freedoms.

The current amendments are listed in the following chart:

The Bill of Rights	
1st	Freedoms of speech, religion, press, assembly, and petition
2nd	Right to bear arms
3rd	Protection against quartering of soldiers
4th	Protection against illegal search and seizure
5th	Right to due process; protection against self-incrimination and double jeopardy
6th	Rights to a speedy trial by jury, to hear accusations and confront the accuser, to witnesses, and to counsel
7th	Right to trial by jury in civil cases
8th	Protection against cruel and unusual punishment
9th	Protects rights not enumerated in the Constitution
10th	Limits the powers of the federal government to those designated in the Constitution

Additional Amendments	
11th	Sovereign immunity
12th	Revision of presidential election procedures
13th	Abolition of slavery
14th	Former slaves granted citizenship; equal protection; due process
15th	Citizens cannot be denied the right to vote based on race, color, or previous condition of servitude
16th	Income tax
17th	Direct election of U.S. Senators
18th	Prohibition of alcohol
19th	Women granted the right to vote
20th	Revision of inauguration date for presidents and vice-presidents
21st	Repeal of the 18th Amendment
22nd	Two-term limit for the presidency
23rd	District of Columbia granted representation in the electoral college
24th	Outlaws the poll tax
25th	Order of succession to the presidency; deals with the situation of presidential disability
26th	Lowers voting age to 18 (from 21)
27th	Delays laws about congressional salaries from going into effect until after the next congressional election

Principles of Democratic Citizenship

A democratic system relies on having citizens who are active participants. Citizens have certain rights and responsibilities to their nation.

In a democracy, the power of the government is limited and the leaders are ultimately responsible to the people. Citizens of the United States aged eighteen and older have the right to vote, which enables them to choose leaders who will represent their interests in the government. Citizens have a responsibility to stay knowledgeable about political issues and to vote according to their conscience to choose the best leaders for the nation.

Citizens can also practice good citizenship by staying politically active, well-informed, and involved in community service and activities. Responsible citizens understand that it takes a group of people working together for a community to function effectively.

Economics is a social science concerned with how goods and services are produced, bought, and sold. Students should understand fundamental economic principles, basic components of economic systems, and the relationship between economics and society.

There are two major division of economics—macroeconomics and microeconomics. **Macroeconomics** is the study of how economics works on a large scale, such as in a whole nation. **Microeconomics** is the study of economics on a smaller scale, looking at the decisions and impacts of individuals, small groups, and specific markets.

Resources are limited (**scarcity**), so people must make choices about how those resources will be allocated. On a small scale, individuals make choices about what they will buy and sell. On a larger scale, societies create economic systems that determine how goods will be produced, bought, and sold and by whom.

Economic Systems

Capitalism is a system in which property and the means of production are privately owned. What is produced, how much, and at what price is dictated by the market forces of **supply and demand**. If demand for a product is high, the supply will run low and prices will increase. If demand is low, the supply will be high and prices will decrease. The **profit motive** encourages hard work and innovation. Capitalism is also called a **market economy**. The purest form of capitalism is **laissez-faire**, in which the government takes a completely hands-off approach to the economic sector and allows market forces to regulate themselves.

Socialism is a system in which property is controlled collectively rather than individually. The purest form of socialism is **communism**, in which everything is owned in common and there is no private property and no social classes. In theory, communism eventually replaces the need for a government. In reality, however, nations that practice forms of communism tend to have very strong governments that take complete economic control. An economy in which the government has total control of the economy through centralized planning is called a **command** or a **planned economy**.

A **mixed economy** is a blend of capitalist and socialist principles, with both publicly and privately owned business operating at the same time.

A **closed economy** is one that is self-sufficient and cut off from outside influences, while an **open economy** allows for trade with other nations.

A **subsistence economy** is one in which people only produce that which is needed to survive.

The Role of the Government in the Economy

Different nations use different economic systems and therefore have different levels of governmental involvement in the economic sectors. A command economy gives the government complete control over economic decision-making, while a laissez-faire system allows the government no role and leaves economic decisions up to individuals and market forces. Most nations' systems are somewhere in the middle of these two extremes.

The United States is primarily a market economy but it does allow the government a degree of regulatory control. The government attempts to intervene in ways that will create a healthy, growing economic environment. Government involvement includes taxation, setting interest rates, regulating the monetary supply, regulating trade, and providing oversight.

Economic Sectors

Different segments of the economy contain different industries that perform different tasks essential to the national economy. All of these sectors are interdependent.

1. Primary sector- draws materials directly from the Earth to be consumed; this includes agriculture, fishing, and mining

2. Secondary sector- manufactures goods out of raw materials; includes industrial work such as making cars or textiles

3. Tertiary sector- service industries, such as retail, childcare, or banking

4. Quaternary sector- research and development

Key Terms

Other important terms in the study of economics include:

- **Balance of trade**- a measure of a nation's exports vs. imports

- **Budget**- planning how current money will be allocated

- **Capital**- resources available for use; may be financial (money), natural, or human (labor)
- **Consumption**- the use of resources
- **Deflation**- an overall decrease in the price of goods and services
- **Depression**- a long period of economic decline, usually marked by inflation, high unemployment, and industrial decline
- **Exports**- goods sold to another country
- **Imports**- goods bought from another country
- **Inflation**- an overall increase in the price of goods and services
- **Profit**- the difference between revenue and cost
- **Recession**- a period of slow economic growth
- **Shortage**- when demand exceeds supply
- **Surplus**- when supply exceeds demand

Types of Resources

There are four major types of resources that factor into economic production. These are:

1. **Natural Resources**- resources acquired from the Earth, such as land, water, minerals, oil, and animals

2. **Human Resources**- people's labor and skills

3. **Capital**- investments in a business such as money, tools, and machinery

4. **Entrepreneurship**- the ability to organize the other three resources to start or grow a business

The Role of Currency

Money is something commonly accepted as a means of payment for goods or services. Money serves three major functions:

1. A means of payment

2. Stored value (you can save up money to accumulate enough value for a future purchase)

3. Unit for measuring how much goods are worth

The monetary system of a particular nation is known as a **currency**. Currencies have different values in relation to one another, which are expressed as **a rate of exchange**.

The value of currency is not completely stable over time. Money gains and loses value as the economy fluctuates.

When money loses value, it is called **inflation**. A dollar, for instance, is worth less than it used to be and consequently, prices go up (inflate). When money gains value, it is called **deflation**.

Scarcity and Choice

Scarcity is the inability to satisfy all wants at the same time. This applies both to individuals and societies. Resources of goods, money, people, and time are limited and choices must be made about how those resources will be used and which wants can be satisfied.

Human populations are greatly affected by the availability of resources. An area must have sufficient resources to sustain its population or the society cannot survive. At the heart of economics are the choices that people and governments make about how to allocate limited resources. Where resources are scarce, people must either obtain resources from outside sources or migrate to areas with sufficient resources. In some cases, societies also work to control the population and limit its growth.

As populations grow and technology becomes more advanced, humanity has used more and more natural resources. As these resources are increasingly scarce, control of resources is important and the trade of resources a vital part of the global economy.

Supply and Demand

Prices are greatly affected by the forces of supply and demand. If a product is in high demand, supplies of that product run low and prices increase. When products are less in demand, there is a greater supply available and prices drop in an effort to sell off the excess merchandise. In this way, consumer spending choices dictate what is produced and the prices that goods sell for.

Competition in the Marketplace

Competition also plays an important role in price. Competition occurs when more than one company is selling the same or a very similar product or service. Competition is typically good for consumers who are given more choices about where to buy their products. Businesses also adjust their prices based on competition. They are competing with each other for a share of the market, and in doing so, tend to lower their prices to entice customers. For this reason, competition tends to drive prices down.

When there is a lack of competition and only one seller controls all or almost all of the market share on a product or service, that is called a **monopoly**. Many governments, including the United States, put measures in place to protect consumers against monopolies, since a monopoly has the potential to drive prices up.

Analysis

Teachers must be able to apply their content knowledge to provide effective classroom instruction.

Test Structure

The Analysis section is the constructed-response portion of Subtest I. This section is worth 25% of your overall score on Subtest I. It will consist of two constructed response questions concerning instructional methods, one related to Reading and Language Arts and one related to Social Studies.

This section of the guide covers the following:

A. General Guidelines and Scoring for Constructed Response Questions

B. Reading and Language Arts Instruction and Assessment

C. Social Studies Instruction and Assessment

The constructed response section of Subtest I consists of two constructed response questions related to instructional methods, one in the area of Reading and Language Arts and one from the area of Social Studies. Questions will present to you a teaching situation and ask you to respond. This could include evaluating student work, presenting one or more methods that could be used to present specific content, assessment methods, or planning instructional goals.

The two constructed response questions together account for 25% of the overall score on Subtest I. They are not timed separately from the multiple choice, so you must pace yourself accordingly. You should plan to spend around 10-15 minutes on each constructed response question.

The constructed response questions are graded according to the following scale, taken from the GACE examination guide:

Score	Description
3	The response is successful in the following ways: • It demonstrates a strong , thorough understanding of the content, pedagogy, and student development relevant to the question. • It answers all parts of the question clearly and specifically. • It shows strong knowledge of content as well as content-specific pedagogy. • It provides strong explanations that are well-supported by examples or details.
2	The response demonstrates some understanding of the topic, but is limited in one or more of the following ways: • It demonstrates a basic, adequate understanding of the content, pedagogy, and student development relevant to the question. • It answers all parts of the question adequately. • It shows adequate knowledge of content as well as content-specific pedagogy. • It provides adequate explanations that are somewhat supported by examples or details.

1	The response is seriously flawed in one or more of the following ways:
	 • It demonstrates a weak, limited understanding of the content, pedagogy, and student development relevant to the question.
	 • It answers the question in a limited way.
	 • It demonstrates one or more of the following weaknesses:
	     o failure to answer most parts of the question
	     o limited knowledge of content and pedagogy
	     o weak explanations inadequately supported by examples or details

0	Response is inappropriate and does not answer the question in one or more of the following ways: • It demonstrates little to no understanding of the content, pedagogy, and student development relevant to the question. • It fails to respond appropriately to any part of the question. • It shows virtually no understanding of content or content-specific pedagogy. • It provides incoherent explanations, no explanations, or no supporting examples

One of the constructed response questions will relate to Reading and Language Arts instruction and/or assessment. You will be presented with a teaching situation and asked to respond in a manner that demonstrates your understanding of content, pedagogy, and student development. This section provides a brief overview of some of the essential elements of Reading and Language Arts instruction and assessment.

Promoting Literacy Skills for Diverse Learners

A diverse student population requires adaptation on the part of the teacher to ensure that the needs of each student are being met. Students come to the classroom with a wide range of backgrounds, prior knowledge, and skills that will result in a classroom whose readers are on many different levels of proficiency.

Some ways to promote literacy skills for a diverse group of learners are:

- Utilizing pre- and post-assessments
- Leveled reading materials
- Scaffolding
- Cooperative learning
- Differentiated assignments and assessments
- Modeling
- Guided practice
- Assessments that vary in form (standardized, portfolio, project-based, anecdotal, performance tasks, etc.)
- Goals based on growths models

Selecting and Using Children's Literature in the Classroom

Literature has a variety of uses in the classroom in addition to being used as a tool for literacy development. It can be used as resource material for research, to create cross-curricular connections between all subject areas, to foster creativity, to model good writing, to promote social development skills, and to foster cross-cultural understanding.

Children's authors work to create literature that is developmentally appropriate, both in reading level and in content. Children's literature is placed into categories according to development level:

- **Early Readers** are targeted for beginning readers and are typically formatted as board books or picture books. These books are usually under 50 pages in length and a have stories written in simple language and supported by illustrations.
- **Middle Grade Readers** include longer books that contain more text and fewer (if any) illustrations than early readers. These also can contain more complex information or plots and more sophisticated vocabulary than early readers. A common format for a middle grade reader is a basic chapter book.
- **Young Adult** literature is aimed at teenage audiences. These are typically longer chapter books whose stories often revolve around teenagers or issues that teenagers typically face.

Choose (or allow children to choose) books that match them both in interest and in appropriateness for their reading level. Aim to choose "just right texts" for most of their reading (rather than those that are easy or so difficult that they lead to much frustration).

Text Response Techniques

An important component of Reading and Language Arts learning is what students do *after* they have read a text—the text response. Students should be encouraged to use a variety of techniques to engage with and respond to the texts they have read. Some types of text response include:

- Think-pair-share discussions
- Keeping a reading response journal
- Artistic response, such as drawing
- Discussion groups such as literature circles
- Graphic organizers
- Learning logs
- Multimedia projects (presentations, videos, web quests, wikis, etc.)
- Conducting further research on the topic they have just read about

Teaching Writing

As students learn the mechanics of writing, it is important to develop their skills at the craft of writing and encourage the increasingly sophisticated use of the components of writing such as organization, vocabulary, word choice, and fluidity.

The best practices for teaching writing involve frequent practice that moves from a high level of support toward independence.

There are four major modes of writing practice in the classroom:

1. **Modeling**- The teacher models writing, demonstrating writing, talking aloud throughout the process, and pointing out skills.

2. **Shared Writing**- The class participates in collaborative writing. The teacher's role is facilitator and scribe.

3. **Guided Practice**- The teacher provides guidance as students do the writing.

4. **Independent Writing**- Students work alone. Teachers provide feedback.

Students should be taught to organize their writing in a logical, coherent manner, according to structures that make sense for the type of writing they are engaging in.

Some ways to encourage writing organization include:

- Teaching story structure and other common structures of writing
- Providing outlines
- Using graphic organizers
- Routine
- Questioning and providing feedback

Common Emergent Literacy Difficulties

Emergent literacy skills are foundational for all future literacy learning. Identifying, preventing, and intervening in emergent literacy difficulties early on can help put students back on track for developing their literacy skills appropriately.

Some of the most common emergent literacy difficulties include:

- Deficits in print awareness, such as not understanding that text should be read from left to right and top to bottom
- "Reading" only the pictures in books without attention to the words
- Lack of alphabetic knowledge and letter-sound correspondence
- Difficulty processing information
- Frustration with not being able to understand text
- Limited vocabulary, which hinders comprehension

- Lack of sight word recognition
- Poor visual-motor integration can hinder writing abilities

When diagnosing and intervening in these and other literacy difficulties, a **Response to Intervention** (RTI) model is often used. RTI is a three-tiered approach that provides interventions for students where needed. The interventions at the lowest level are available to all students as they develop their skills. Those who do not respond to the basic level are given second-tier interventions. Those few who still do not respond receive more specialized, intensive interventions on the third tier. The system is based on frequent progress monitoring and data analysis.

Some strategies that can be used within the classroom to prevent and intervene in common emergent literacy difficulties include:

- Direct instruction
- Modeling
- Provided leveled readers
- Matching students with "just right" texts for most of their reading (rather than those that are easy or so difficult that they lead to much frustration)
- Building vocabulary
- Phonics instruction
- Improving concentration by minimizing distractions
- Frequently reading aloud
- Choosing books (or allowing students to choose books) that match students' interests
- Partner reading

Types of Assessments

In order to properly determine a student's level of learning, assessments should be frequent and varied in form. Assessments can be categorized as either formative or summative and as either formal or informal.

Formative assessments occur "in the midst" of learning, before a subject or skill is expected to be mastered. These checks of progress along the way help to ensure that students are on the right track and can be used to make adjustments in instruction. **Summative assessments** occur at the end of a specified learning period, such as a unit or a school year. They are meant to assess what the student has learned overall.

Formal assessments are structured assessments based around data that follow certain guidelines. There are many types of formal assessments. They include:

- **Criterion-referenced tests**- assessments in which a student's achievement is measured against a set of pre-determined criteria

- **Norm-referenced tests**- assessments in which a student's performance is measured against the performance of other students; results often shown as a bell curve or as a percentile

- **Curriculum-based tests**- assessments based on students' performance in the local curriculum as a means of gathering information about their learning and to make instructional decisions

- **Diagnostic tests**- assessments used to identify weaknesses in learning, to assess current levels of knowledge, or to identify learning problems

- **Intelligence tests**- assessments designed to test the natural ability to think and reason (rather than testing learned knowledge)

- **Teacher-generated instruments**- assessments created by the individual classroom teacher to align with instructional goals for lessons, units, or periods of time (i.e. semester, school year)

Informal assessments use methods other than standardized instruments to gather information on students' learning. Some types of informal assessment include:

- **Observation**- watching students with a purpose

- **Anecdotal record**- a brief description of observed student behavior

- **Running record**- keeping track of behaviors or events over time for individual students

- **Work sample**- a piece of student work kept as an indicator of learning

- **Portfolio**- a collection of work samples and other products from a particular student to document achievement over time

- **Reading-specific assessments**- Informal assessments specifically designed to assess reading skills include comprehension checks, story retelling, fluency checks, and reading inventories

Evaluating the Appropriateness of Assessments

For an assessment to be effective, it has to be an accurate measure of the students' skills. The two main measures of a test's appropriateness are reliability and validity.

- **Reliability** means that a test is consistent across multiple measurements.
- **Validity** means that the test actually measures what it claims to measure.

To be considered accurate, a test must be both reliable and valid.

Analyzing and Utilizing Assessment Data

Assessment data has many uses. It can inform students, parents, teachers, and others of how well a student is performing. It can also be used to guide instructional practices and to make educational decisions. Where literacy levels and skills vary amongst students in a single classroom, instruction should be differentiated to meet the needs of individual students.

Screening is an evaluation done at the beginning of the year that is intended to assess the student's reading level and capabilities. This information can then be used to make goals and inform instruction for the year.

Progress monitoring is used throughout the year to show gains and document achievement, as well as assess the effectiveness of instruction. The data collected from progress monitoring can be used to adjust instruction to better meet the student's literacy needs.

Many of the types of formal and informal assessments listed in the previous section could be used for screening or progress monitoring purposes.

Sharing the results of screening and progress monitoring throughout the school year with students, parents, and other stakeholders can help to set goals and make educational decisions. When presenting assessment data, be sure to explain thoroughly what the data means. For example, ensure that everyone looking at norm-referenced data understands the difference between a percentile and a percentage score.

Selecting Classroom Organizational Formats

In the classroom, there are many possible organizational schemes which lend themselves to different types of activities and learning. When selecting an organizational format, the teacher should bear in mind the objective of the lesson and choose the format which will be most conducive to achievement of the lesson goals.

Some common organizational structures with the Language Arts classroom are:

- Small groups that work on a task then present their findings to the class

- Partner work

- Literature circles- small, temporary groups in which students discuss literary texts

- Literacy stations or centers- students move to different areas of the classroom where they engage in different literacy activities, such as writing, reading, vocabulary, text response, listening, etc.

- Workshops- teacher models and then the students engage in guided practice

One of the constructed response questions will relate Social Studies instruction and/or assessment. You will be presented with a teaching situation and asked to respond in a manner that demonstrates your understanding of content, pedagogy, and student development. This section provides a brief overview of some of the essential elements of Social Studies instruction and assessment.

Learning Environments for Social Studies

Creating a environment conducive to learning, exploration, and cooperation is essential for the social science classroom. This can involve both the physical structures of the room and the organizational formats used in lessons.

It is important that the physical classroom be set up for learning by cultivating interest and encouraging exploration of social science concepts. Some ways of physically preparing the classroom include:

- Displaying maps, timelines, and other images related to the study of social science
- Making displays specific to the current social science topics
- Providing a resource area with books, newspapers, and other tools for social science investigation
- Creating a word wall of social science vocabulary
- Displaying student work

In the classroom, there are many possible organizational schemes which lend themselves to different types of activities and learning. When selecting an organizational format, the teacher should bear in mind the objective of the lesson and choose the format which will be most conducive to achievement of the lesson goals.

Some common organizational structures with the social science classroom are:

- Partners or mall groups that work on a task then present their findings Stations or centers- students move to different areas of the classroom where they engage in different activities
- Workshops- teacher models and then the students engage in guided practice
- Independent work

Types of General Assessments

In order to determine whether or not students are progressing in their skills, assessment is necessary. Selecting the appropriate assessments that match instructional objectives is essential for evaluating whether or not students are meeting those objectives and for adjustment of instructional practices.

The major types of assessments that can apply to any subject area are explored in the previous section ("Reading and Language Arts Instruction and Assessment"). Refer to that section for more details on the types of tests listed below, as well as for information on analyzing and utilizing assessment data to guide classroom instruction.

Common formal assessments include:

- Criterion-referenced tests
- Norm-referenced tests
- Curriculum-based tests
- Diagnostic tests
- Teacher-generated instruments

Common informal assessments include:

- Observation
- Anecdotal record
- Running record
- Work sample
- Portfolio

Social Studies Assessments

Some specific types of assessments that are commonly used in the area of Social Studies include:

- Map skills assessments
- Document-based questions
- Timelines
- Essays, reports, or presentations

Mathematics

Knowledge of mathematics is foundational for student success. Students develop skills in mathematical problem-solving that transfer to many real world applications and career fields.

Test Structure

The Mathematics section makes up 53% of Subtest II. Within this section, there are six major subcategories with which you must be familiar:

A. Counting and Cardinality

B. Numbers and Operations

C. Algebraic Thinking

D. Fractions

E. Measurement and Data

F. Geometry

Each subcategory is divided into topics, which state the skills you must be able to demonstrate on the exam.

Counting and Cardinality

Some of the earliest mathematical skills a child needs involve connecting numbers with quantities and being able to count, compare, and order those quantities.

Topics Addressed:

1. The Development of Numerical Skills

Long before they have a math class, young children begin to formulate math-related reasoning. These early ideas are known as **prenumeration concepts**.

One such concept is the **meaning of number**. Children learn that numbers refer to quantities of something. Once they understand this, they can begin to count.

Informal counting is one of the first mathematical procedures a child learns. Once kids learn their numbers in sequence, they can begin to associate those numbers with objects and they will begin to point and count at the same time.

Young children can also begin to see **patterns** among objects. Recognizing groupings as patterns will eventually develop into higher level mathematical skills as students learn to recognize patterns in numbers and in geometry.

Another early concept is that of **relative magnitude**. This is the ability to make comparisons and determine whether one number is larger or smaller than another. They can then begin to order things based on size or quantity.

Numbers and Operations

This section covers number theory, the four major operations, and basic mathematical concepts and strategies which will lay the foundation for students' future mathematical learning.

Topics Addressed:

1. Number Systems and Place Value
2. Numerical Operations
3. Properties of Numbers and Operations
4. Factors and Multiples

Basic Number Systems

There are several basic categories of numbers.

- **Natural numbers** are those numbers we typically use to count (1, 2, 3...)

- **Whole numbers** are the natural numbers and zero (0, 1, 2, 3...)

- **Integers** are whole numbers and their corresponding negatives (.. -3, -2, -1, 0, 1, 2, 3...)

- **Fractions** are portions of integers, expressed with a numerator and a denominator

  (¼, ½, etc.)

- **Decimals** are portions of integers, expressed as numbers following a decimal point

  (0.5, 0.67, etc.)

- **Even numbers** are integers divisible by two (...-6, -4, -2, 2, 4, 6...)

- **Odd numbers** are integers not divisible by two(... -7, -5, -3, 3, 5, 7...)

- **Rational numbers** are all integers and fractions

- **Irrational numbers** are any numbers that cannot be expressed as fractions, such as an infinite, non-repeating decimal

- **Exponents** are numbers that raise another number to a power, making it multiply by itself a certain number of times (3^2 = 3 x 3 = 9, etc.)

- **Roots-** the root of a number x is another number such that when the number is multiplied by itself a given number of times, it equals x ($\sqrt{4}$ = 2, etc.)

Place Value

Place value is a way of organizing numbers based on groupings of ten. The place value in which a digit lays conveys how many groups of ten (or one hundred, or one thousand, etc.) it represents. Place value is also used in decimals.

Whole Numbers						
Millions	Hundred Thousands	Ten Thousands	Thousands	Hundreds	Tens	Units
1,000,000	100,000	10,000	1,000	100	10	1
2,478,390	2,**4**78,390	2,4**7**8,390	2,47**8**,390	2,478,**3**90	2,478,3**9**0	2,478,39**0**

Decimals					
Tenths	Hundredths	Thousandths	Ten Thousandths	Hundred Thousandths	Millionths
.1	.01	.001	.0001	.00001	.000001
.**2**37894	.2**3**7894	.23**7**894	.237**8**94	.2378**9**4	.23789**4**

Estimation and Rounding

Estimation provides a close guess as to a value. An exact number is not always necessary and estimation can be a time-saving skill for everyday calculations such as product costs, how much should be left for a tip, and quantity estimations.

One type of estimation is **rounding**, which is arriving at a close value to a given number based on place value. You can round to any place value.

The rule for rounding is to look one place to the right of the place value you want to round to. If that digit is five or higher, round up. If it is less than five, round down.

Example:

Number	Roundest to the Nearest Ten	Rounded to the Nearest Hundred	Rounded to the Nearest Thousand
3,583	3,580	3,600	4,000
6,149	6,150	6,100	6,000

Scientific Notation and Expanded Form

There are also different ways to write out the same number so that it looks different and is in a standardized form. Scientific notation and expanded form are two different ways of writing numbers that are both based on place value in a base-ten system

Scientific notation puts all numbers in a standard form by changing them so that there is only one place value before a decimal point and then the number is written in terms of multiplication by 10 to a power.

Examples: 321 becomes 3.21×10^2

2,250.75 becomes 2.25075×10^3

0.62 becomes 6.2×10^{-1}

Expanded form breaks a number up into an addition expression based on the place value of each digit.

Examples: 748 becomes 700 + 40 + 8

2,389 becomes 2,000 + 300 + 80 + 9

Translating Mathematical Language

Mathematical problem-solving requires knowledge of such concepts as representation, variables, and arithmetic operations. In order to solve problems, students will need to be comfortable with the vocabulary associated with the arithmetic operations. This is especially important in word problems where students will need to deduce the operation necessary to solve without being able to see the symbol for the operation.

Addition	Subtraction	Multiplication	Division
Add	Subtract	Multiply	Divide
Sum	Difference	Product	Quotient
More than	Less than	Total	Distribute
Plus	Minus	Times	Per
In addition	Diminished		
Increased	Decreased		
All together	Remove		
Total	Take away		
And	Deduct		

Equivalence

Equivalence is being equal in value. The same value can take on many different forms. For example. a fraction can also be expressed as a decimal that is equal in value.

Many mathematical situations will require students to work with the concept of equivalence and to translate from one equivalent form of a number to another. This can include generating equivalent fractions; simplifying expressions; and converting between fractions, decimals, and percents.

Example:

Fraction(s)	Decimal	Percent
$\frac{1}{4}, \frac{2}{8}$, etc.	0.25	25%
$\frac{1}{2}, \frac{2}{4}$, etc.	0.5	50%

The four basic operations—addition, subtraction, multiplication, and division—serve as the basis for all mathematical processes.

Addition

Addition is bringing two or more numbers (or objects) together to make a new total called a **sum**. A common method used in addition is regrouping by carrying. When adding vertically, add each place value individually, starting on the right and moving left. If any single place value sums to a number greater than 10, keep the value over 10 in that place value and carry the tens place to the next column to be added into that place value.

Example

```
  25
  18
+ 11
```

```
  25
  18
+ 11
```
First, add the ones place column.

```
  1
  25
  18
+ 11
  54
```
The sum of those numbers is 14, which is larger than 10. To regroup, write the 4 in the ones column of the answer space, and move the 1 to the tens place. It will be added in there for a total of 54.

Subtraction

Subtraction is taking numbers (or objects) away from a group to create a new total, called a **difference**. A common method used in subtraction is regrouping by borrowing. When subtracting vertically, subtract each place value individually, moving from right to left. If ever the top number (the one you are subtracting *from*) is smaller than the bottom number (the one being subtracted), you will need to borrow. To borrow, add 10 to the digit you were trying to subtract from, then subtract 1 from the next place to the left to compensate.

Example

```
  62
- 17
```

```
  62
- 17
```
Start with the ones column.

```
  12
  62
- 17
   5
```
Notice that the 2 is not large enough to subtract the 7 from it. This means we will need to borrow.

```
 5 12
  62
- 17
  45
```
Borrow from the tens column by subtracting 1 from the top number, making the 6 into a 5. Then subtract the tens column. The answer is 45.

Multiplication

Multiplication is adding a number to itself a certain number of times. It is ultimately a shortcut to repeated addition. Multiplication quantifies equal groups of things.

The two numbers in a multiplication problem are called the multiplicand and the multiplier. The answer is called the **product**. The typical process for multiplication involves multiplying the multiplicand by each digit of the multiplier, then adding the results to get the product.

Example

```
  42
x 13
```

```
  42
x 13
 126
```
Start by multiplying the multiplicand (42) by the ones place of the multiplier. 4 x 3 = 12 and 2 x 3 =6

```
  42
x 13
 126
 420
```
Then, multiply 42 by the tens place of the multiplier, using a 0 to hold the place value in   the ones.

2 x 1 = 2 and 4 x 1 = 4

```
  42
x 13
 126
+420
 546
```
Finally, add these results to get the final product of 546.

Division

Division is splitting a number into equal groups. The number being divided is the **dividend**, the number it is divided by is the **divisor**, and the answer is the **quotient**.

In division, dividing moves in place values from left to right. Any leftovers that do not divide evenly into the dividend become either a remainder, fraction, or decimal.

Example

```
5⟌257
```

```
   5
5|257
```

In this   example, 257 is the dividend and 5 is the divisor. Move
from left   to right in the place values of the dividend. 5 cannot divide
into 2.

```
    5
5⟌257
```

Expand to the right and look at the first two digits, 25.

5 *does* divide evenly into 25 (5 times).

```
   51 R2
5⟌257
  -5
   2
```

Now, move to the right again. 5 goes into 7 with a remainder of 2. To divide without remainders, you would add on decimal places until the division comes out evenly. In this case, the result would be 51.4

Note: There are many methods for division other than the long division shown, but the basic elements are still the same.

Modeling the Four Operations

Addition and Subtraction Models

Addition can be modeled as a "**put-together**" problem, with either an unknown addend or an unknown sum. Visual models can be used to show the parts being put together to form a total.

Example: *There are 2 oranges and 3 bananas in a fruit bowl. How many pieces of fruit are there all together?*

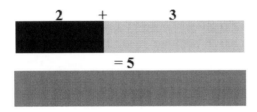

There are 5 pieces of fruit all together.

Subtraction can be modeled as a "**take-apart**" problem, with either an unknown minuend, an unknown subtrahend, or an unknown difference. Visual models can be used to show that subtraction means splitting a whole into component parts.

Example: *8 students were asked whether they like dogs or cats better. 5 students picked dogs. How many students picked cats?*

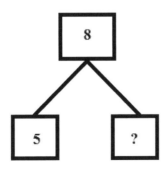

3 students picked cats.

Multiplication and Area Models

An **array** is one way to model a multiplication problem visually. One factor is shown vertically and the other horizontally.

Example: 4 x 3 = 12 can be modeled as an array like this:

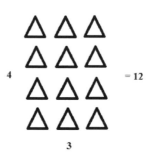

This can also be used to relate to calculating the area of rectangles as it is similar to **tiling**, wherein a rectangle is divided into unit squares which can be counted to find the area.

Example: To find the area of a rectangle that measures 8 units by 4 units using tiling, divide the rectangle into unit squares and count them to find the area.

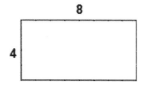 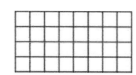

$8 \times 4 = 32$ units^2

Division Models

There are two main types of division problems:

- **Measurement division** is needed when students know how many objects are in each group but do not know how many groups there are

- **Partitive division** is needed when students know how many groups there need to be but not how many objects will be in each group

Visual models can be used to understand either type of division problem as splitting objects into equal groupings.

Example: *Jason is placing 6 cookies into bags to keep them fresh. If he puts 3 cookies in each bag, how many bags will he fill?*

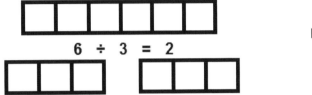

He will fill 2 bags.

The Commutative, Distributive, and Associative Properties

Basic operations have special properties that govern how they work and can make them easier to solve.

Property	Applies To	Description	Example
Commutative Property	Addition and Multiplication	The order of the numbers being added or multiplied does not affect final result	1 + 3 = 3 + 1 2 x 5 = 5 x 2
Distributive Property	Multiplication	$a(b + c) = ab + ac$ Multiplication in front of parenthesis can be distributed to each term within the parentheses.	2(3+1) = 2 x 3 + 2 x 1 = 6 + 2 = 8 This yields the same result as 2(3+1) = 2(4) = 8
Associative Property	Addition and Multiplication	If the operations are all the same (all addition or all multiplication) the terms can be regrouped by moving the parentheses. $(a + b) + c = a + (b + c)$ $a(bc) = (ab)c$	Addition: (1 + 2) + 3 = 3 + 3 = 6 1 + (2 + 3) = 1 + 5 = 6 Multiplication: 3(4y) = 12y (3 x 4)y = 12y

Order of Operations

When an equation has more than one of these operations in it, the operations must be performed in a certain order. The order can be remembered with the acronym PEMDAS, which stands for:

- **Parentheses**- Complete any operations enclosed within parentheses first. If more than one operation is inside the parentheses, perform the operations within the parentheses in PEMDAS order, then proceed with the operations outside the parentheses.

- **Exponents**- Deal with any exponents next.

- **Multiplication/Division**- Multiplication and division can be done in the same step as one another.

- **Addition/Subtraction**- Addition and subtraction can be done in the same step as one another.

Special Properties of Zero and One

Zero and one have their own special properties that no other numbers possess.

Properties of Zero

- *Addition property of zero*- Adding 0 to a number does not change the number's value.

  $x + 0 = x$

- *Multiplication property of zero*- Any number multiplied by 0 equals 0

  $0x = 0$

- *Additive inverse*- The sum of any number and its additive inverse is 0

  $x + -x = 0$

- *Powers of zero*- 0 raised to any power equals 0

  $0^x = 0$

- *Zero as a dividend*- Dividing 0 by any number results in a quotient of 0

  $0 \div x = 0$

- *Division by zero*- Dividing any number by 0 results in a quotient that is undefined

  $x \div 0 = undefined$

Properties of One

1. *Multiplication property of one-* Multiplying a number by 1 does not change the number's value.

    $1 x = x$

2. *Multiplicative inverse-* The product of any number and its multiplicative inverse is 1

    $x(\frac{1}{x}) = 1$

3. *Powers of one-* 1 raised to any power equals 1

    $1^x = 1$

4. *Quotient of one-* Any number (other than 0) divided by itself equals 1

    $x \div x = 1$

Additive and Multiplicative Inverses

An **additive inverse** of a number is its equal opposite such that when the two are added together, they will equal 0. For example:

Number	Additive Inverse
1	-1
-25	25
x	$-x$

The **multiplicative inverse** of a number is the reciprocal of the number such that when the two are multiplied, they equal 1. For example:

Number	Multiplicative Inverse
5	1/5
1/2	2
x	1/x

Absolute Value

A related concept is that of **absolute value**, a number's distance from 0. Absolute value is always positive. If the number is greater than 0, it is its own absolute value. If negative, its additive inverse (the positive equivalent of itself) is its absolute value. For example:

Number	Absolute Value
5	5
-10	10
x	x
$-x$	x

Laws of Exponents

The following chart lays out the basic rules governing the use of exponents.

Types of Laws	Law	Example
Product Rules	$a^n \cdot a^m = a^{n+m}$	$2^2 \cdot 2^3 = 2^{2+3} = 32$
	$a^n \cdot b^n = (a \cdot b)^n$	$2^2 \cdot 3^2 = (2 \cdot 3)^2 = 36$
Quotient Rules	$a^n / a^m = a^{n-m}$	$2^5 / 2^3 = 2^{5-3} = 4$
	$a^n / b^n = (a / b)^n$	$4^3 / 2^3 = (4/2)^3 = 8$
Power Rules	$(b^n)^m = b^{n \cdot m}$	$(2^3)^4 = 2^{3 \cdot 4} = 4096$
	$^m\sqrt{(b^n)} = b^{n/m}$	$^2\sqrt{(2^4)} = 2^{4/2} = 4$
Negative Exponents	$b^{-n} = 1 / b^n$	$2^{-3} = 1/2^3 = 0.125$
Zero Rules	$b^0 = 1$	$9^0 = 1$
	$0^n = 0$, for $n>0$	$0^3 = 0$
One Rules	$b^1 = b$	$7^1 = 7$
	$1^n = 1$	$1^4 = 1$

Factors

Factors are whole numbers that are multiplied together to get a product.

Example: The factors of 16 are 1, 2, 4, 8, and 16.

The processing of breaking a number down into its factors is called **factoring**.

Prime and Composite Numbers

Whole numbers can be classified by how many factors they have as either being prime or composite numbers.

- **Prime numbers** are those numbers (other than zero and one) that have only two factors—themselves and 1

  2, 3, 5, 7, 11…

- **Composite numbers** are any positive integers that are not prime, meaning they have more than two factors

  4, 6, 8, 9, 10…

Prime factorization involves factoring a number and then factoring the factors, if necessary, until all factors are prime and multiply together to equal the original number. One way of performing prime factorization is by using a **factor tree**.

Example: The prime factorization of 24 is 3 x 2 x 2 x 2.

Greatest Common Factor

When comparing the factors of two numbers, the largest factor that they have in common in called the **Greatest Common Factor (GCF)**.

Example:

- Factors of 20: 1, 2, **4**, 5, 10, 20
- Factors of 24: 1, 2, 3, **4**, 6, 8, 12, 24

    GCF: 4

Multiples

Multiples are the result of multiplying a number by whole numbers.

Example:

- The multiples of 4 are 4, 8, 12, 16, 20, 24...

Least Common Multiple

When comparing the multiples of two numbers, the smallest multiple that they have in common is called the **Least Common Multiple (LCM)**.

Example:

- Multiples of 3: 3, 6, 9, 12, **15**, 18, 21...
- Multiples of 5: 5, 10, **15**, 20, 25, 30...

    LCM: 15

Algebraic Thinking

Algebra is a branch of mathematics that uses variables to represent numbers. At the elementary level, students are introduced to basic concepts that will be foundational when they move on to study algebra in greater depth later in their academic careers. This section covers recognizing, creating, and predicting patterns; functions; and the application of basic algebraic concepts to solve mathematical and real world problems.

Topics Addressed:

1. Algebraic Concepts
2. Ratios, Proportions, and Percents
3. Functions and Patterns

Algebraic Language

Variables

A variable is a letter used to refer to an unknown quantity. Algebraic problem solving often requires solving to find the value of a variable.

Example: $2x = 12$

$x = 6$

Expressions

Expressions are mathematical phrases that can contain numbers, variables, and operations.

Equations

Equations are two mathematical expressions that are set equal to one another using an equals sign (=). An equation can also be called an **equality**.

When solving equations for a variable, operations performed to one side must be performed to the other.

There are several properties of equalities:

4. Reflexive property- Every number is equal to itself.

   $x = x$

5. Symmetric property- If a number is equal to another number, then the converse is also true.

   If $x = y$ then $y = x$.

6. Transitive property- If number a is equal to number b, and number b is equal to number c, then number a is also equal to number c.

   If $x = y$ and $y = z$, then $x = z$.

7. Substitution property- If two numbers are equal to one another, they are interchangeable.

   If $x = y$, then $x + z = y + z$

8. Property of addition, subtraction, multiplication, and division- If two numbers are equal, they will remain equal if the same number is added to or subtracted from them, or if they are multiplied or divided by the same number.

If $x = y$, then $x + z = y + z$ If $x = y$, then $xz = yz$

If $x = y$, then $x - z = y - z$ If $x = y$, then $x/z = y/z$

Inequalities

An **inequality** is a comparison of two expressions. The two sides of the equation are separated by one of the following symbols:

9. $<$ *less than*

10. $>$ *greater than*

11. $\leq$ *less than or equal to*

12. $\geq$ *greater than or equal to*

When solving inequalities for a variable, operations performed to one side must be performed to the other. When adding or subtracting the same value from both sides, or when multiplying or dividing by a positive number on both sides, the inequality sign does not change. When multiplying or dividing by a negative number, the inequality sign is reversed.

Formulas

Formulas are standard equations with variables that follow specific rules and are used to solve specific types of problems. Below are several examples of fundamental algebraic formulas.

- Difference of two perfect squares

$a^2 - b^2 = (a + b)(a - b)$

- Quadratic formula- a method of solving a quadratic equation ($ax^2 + bx + c = 0$)

$$x = \frac{-b \pm \sqrt{b^2 - 4ac}}{2a}$$

- Pythagorean theorem- used to find a missing length of a right triangle

$$a^2 + b^2 = c^2$$

- Distance formula- used to measure the distance between two points on a coordinate plane

$$d = \sqrt{(x_2 - x_1)^2 + (y_2 - y_1)^2}$$

- Midpoint formula- used to find the midpoint between two points on a coordinate plane

$$\left(\frac{(x_2 + x_1)}{2}, \frac{(y_2 + y_1)}{2} \right)$$

- Slope formula- used to find the slope of a line on a coordinate plane

$$m = \frac{y_2 - y_1}{x_2 - x_1}$$

- Slope intercept formula- the equation of a straight line

$y = mx + b$ where m is the slope and b is the y-intercept

Ratios, Proportions, and Percents

Ratios

A **ratio** is a way to compare two numbers.

> Example: If a parent has one son and three daughters, the ratio of sons to daughters would be one to three.

A ratio can be expressed in words, as a fraction, or as two numbers separated by a colon. The ratio "one to three" is the same as "$\frac{1}{3}$" is the same as "1:3."

Proportions

A **proportion** is two ratios set equal to each other. Proportions are often expressed as two fractions with an equals sign between them.

> Example: $\frac{1}{3} = \frac{2}{6}$

Proportions that include an unknown can be solved by cross-multiplying.

> Example: The ratio of cats to dogs in a pet is 3 to 2. If there are 12 cats, how many dogs are there?
>
> $\frac{3}{2} = \frac{12}{x}$
>
> $3x = 12 \times 2$
>
> $3x = 24$
>
> $x = 8$
>
> There are 8 dogs in the pet store.

Percents

Percents convey a ratio out of 100. Percents are represented with a percentage symbol (%). The percentage formula is:

$$\frac{\%}{100} = \frac{part}{whole}$$

It is solved by cross-multiplying.

Example: What is 20% of 50?

$$\frac{20}{100} = \frac{x}{50}$$

$100x = 1,000$

$x = 10$

Functions

Functions are algebraic equations that have an input (*x*) and an output (*f(x)*). In a function, each input value corresponds with exactly one output value. At the elementary level, functions are often expressed using tables and are then sometimes graphed.

Example:

Input	Output
2	5
3	6
15	18
21	24

Rule: Add 3

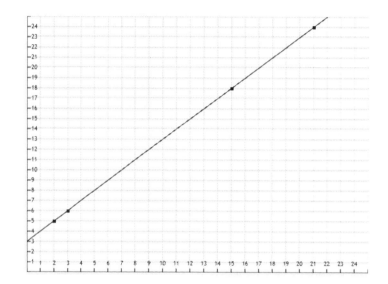

You can tell whether or not a graph shows a function by using the **vertical line test**. If a vertical line would only pass through the graph once, it is a function.

Functions whose data points form a straight-line graph are known as **linear functions**. Those that do not form a straight line are called **non-linear functions**.

Numerical Patterns

Numerical patterns are sets of numbers that follow a rule that governs the relationship between the numbers and dictates what number will come next in the set. Numerical patterns require students to analyze a set of numbers, discover the relationship between them, and articulate the pattern as a general rule that will work to the *n*th term in the series. Some examples of common number patterns are:

Pattern Name	Description	Example
Arithmetic Sequence	The same value is added each time	1, 5, 9, 13, 17, 21... (add 4 each time)
Geometric Sequence	The same value is multiplied each time	1, 3, 9, 27, 81... (multiply by 3 each time)
Squares	Square each number (n^2)	1, 4, 9, 16, 25...
Cubes	Cube each number (n^3)	1, 8, 27, 64, 125...
Fibonacci Sequence	Each number is the sum of the two numbers before it	0, 1, 1, 2, 3, 5, 8, 13, 21...
Triangular Sequence	Each number adds what would be another row to a triangle of dots $x_n = n(n+1)/2$	 A numerical example of a triangular sequence: 1, 3, 6, 10, 15, 21, 28, 36...

Shape Patterns

Patterns in shapes may involve shape, size, color, rotation, or other physical attributes of the shapes used to create a recognizable pattern. Students will be expected to articulate, predict, and create shape patterns.

Two common types of shape patterns are patterns of repetition and patterns of symmetry.

Patterns of repetition involve the repetition of elements in a predictable sequence.

Patterns of symmetry have a line of symmetry which creates a mirror image within the pattern.

Fractions

Fractions represent partial integers. Students should be able to understand, represent, compare, and perform operations with fractions.

Topics Addressed:

1. Understanding Fractions
2. Performing Operations on Fractions

Fractions are used to represent a part of a whole. **Integers** are numbers that do not contain fractional parts (whole numbers and their negatives).

Students should have an understanding of the meaning of fractions and be able to solve problems with the four basic operations involving fractions.

Representing Fractions

Visuals are often used to help students understand fractions. Creating a visual representation of a fraction involves splitting a whole into equivalent parts and indicating (usually through shading) some of those parts as the fractional pieces.

Example: $\frac{1}{4}$ can be represented as the shape below, which is split into four equal parts with one of them shaded.

Students can be taught that the selected area represents the numerator of the fraction, and the total number of pieces represents the denominator of the fraction.

Improper Fractions and Mixed Numbers

When a fraction has a value that is greater than 1, it can either be expressed as an improper fraction or a mixed number.

An improper fraction has a numerator greater than the denominator (e.g., $\frac{22}{7}$).

A mixed number contains both a whole number and a fraction (e.g., $1\frac{1}{3}$).

To convert an improper fraction to a mixed number, divide the numerator by the denominator. The whole number portion of the quotient becomes the whole number of the mixed number, the remainder becomes the numerator of the new fraction, and the denominator remains the same.

Example: $\frac{22}{7} = 3\frac{1}{7}$

To convert a mixed number to an improper fraction, multiply the denominator by the whole number and add the numerator. This total becomes the new numerator and the denominator remains the same.

Example: $1\frac{1}{3} = \frac{4}{3}$

Adding and Subtracting Fractions

To add and subtract fractions with like denominators, leave the denominator alone and add or subtract the numerators.

Example: $\frac{1}{5} + \frac{3}{5} = \frac{4}{5}$

To add or subtract fractions with unlike denominators, change the fractions to equivalent ones with a common denominator, then add or subtract the numerators.

Example: $\frac{1}{5} + \frac{2}{3} =$

$$\frac{3}{15} + \frac{10}{15} = \frac{13}{15}$$

Multiplying and Dividing Fractions

To multiply fractions, multiply across, combining the numerators to form a new numerator and the denominators to form a new denominator.

Example: $\frac{1}{4} \times \frac{3}{5} = \frac{3}{20}$

To divide fractions, change the second fraction to its reciprocal (switch the numerator and denominator) and multiply.

Example: $\frac{2}{3} \div \frac{3}{5} =$

$$\frac{2}{3} \times \frac{5}{3} = \frac{10}{9} \ (or \ 1\frac{1}{9})$$

Comparing Fractions

When comparing fractions with like denominators, the fraction with the larger numerator has the greater value.

Example: $\frac{2}{3} > \frac{1}{3}$

When comparing fractions with the same numerator but different denominators, the fraction with the smaller denominator has the greater value.

Example: $\frac{2}{3} > \frac{2}{5}$

When comparing fractions that have neither the same numerators nor denominators, convert the fractions so that they have a common denominator and then compare the numerators as before.

Example: To compare $\frac{3}{4}$ and $\frac{2}{3}$, first change the fractions so that they have a common denominator, then compare the numerators.

$\frac{9}{12} > \frac{8}{12}$ therefore $\frac{3}{4} > \frac{2}{3}$.

Measurement and Data

Students learn to measure and interpret data using different systems and forms of representation.

Topics Addressed:

1. Measurement Systems
2. Representing and Interpreting Data

Students will learn to understand measurement concepts using different sets of units. The three main types of units students will encounter are nonstandard, customary, and metric units.

Nonstandard Measurement

Nonstandard measurement is how elementary students first learn to measure. The use of nonstandard units often involves measuring using small objects such as paper clips.

Customary Measurement

Customary measurement is the primary system of measurement used in the United States. There are customary units to measure length, weight, volume, temperature, and time.

Length is measured in inches, feet, yards, and miles using measuring tools such as rulers and measuring tapes.

- 12 inches (in. or ") = 1 foot (ft. or ')
- 36 inches = 3 feet = 1 yard (yd.)
- 5,280 feet = 1,760 yards = 1 mile (mi.)

Weight is measured in ounces, pounds, and tons using a scale.

- 16 ounces (oz.) = 1 pound (lb.)
- 1,000 pounds = 1 ton (T.)

Volume is measured in fluid ounces, cups, pints, quarts, and gallons using a measuring cup, beaker, or other marked container for holding liquid.

- 8 fluid ounces (fl. oz.) = 1 cup (c.)
- 16 fluid ounces = 2 cups = 1 pint (pt.)

- 4 cups = 2 pints = 1 quart (qt.)
- 8 pints = 4 quarts = 1 gallon (gal.)

Temperature is measured in degrees Fahrenheit (ºF) using a thermometer.

Time is measured in seconds, minutes, and hours using a clock.

- 60 seconds (sec.) = 1 minute (min.)
- 60 minutes = 1 hour (hr.)

Metric Measurement

The metric system of measurement is used in most of the world. It is based on units that are multiples of ten. No matter what is being measured, the units have prefixes which tell you the size of the unit relative to the others of its type.

The basic unit for each form of measurement is:

- Length- meter
- Mass- gram
- Volume- liter

Adding one of the prefixes in the chart below changes the value.

Kilo-	Hecto-	Deka-	Unit	Deci-	Centi-	Milli-
.001	.01	.1	1	10	100	1000

For example, this means that 1 gram is equal to 1000 milligrams. To convert between units in the metric system, simply use this chart to determine how many places to move the decimal.

The metric system has two scales for measuring temperature—Celsius (ºC) and Kelvin (K).

Precision and Accuracy

Precision and accuracy are ways of describing measurement data.

Precision is how close a measured value is to an actual (true) value.

Accuracy is how close measured values are to each other.

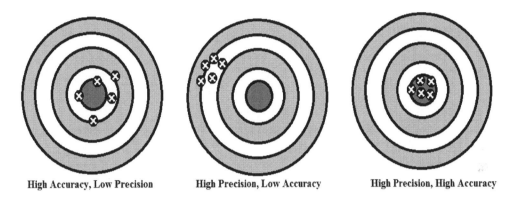

High Accuracy, Low Precision   High Precision, Low Accuracy   High Precision, High Accuracy

Graphic Representations

Quantitative information can be displayed visually with the use of charts and graphs. There are several common types of charts and graphs with which elementary students should be familiar.

Pictographs

Pictographs use pictures or symbols to represent pieces of data. A symbol may represent one item or a key may indicate that each symbol represents more than one item. Quantities of each item are obtained by counting the symbols.

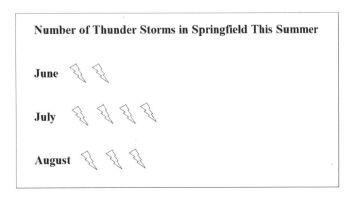

Bar Graphs

Bar graphs use bars to represent quantities. The quantity represented by each bar is obtained by reading the height of the bar.

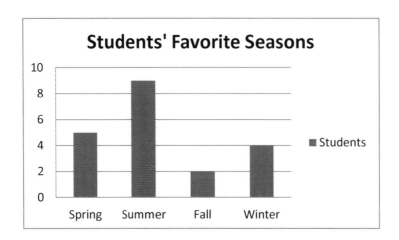

Pie Graphs

Pie graphs are used to show information in relation to a whole. The circle represents a whole and is divided into segments to represent the portions. The portions are usually shown in percentages.

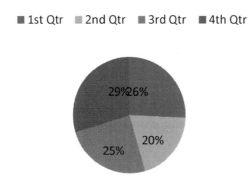

Line Graphs

Line graphs use lines to connect data points and are used to show change over time.

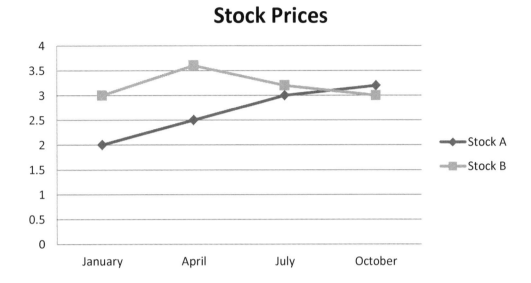

Descriptive Statistics

Descriptive statistics are used to explain patterns and relationships among sets of data. The basic types of descriptive statistics include mean, median, mode, range, and frequency distribution.

Mean

Mean is another word for average. To find the mean of a set of numbers, add the numbers together and divide the sum by how many numbers there are.

Example:

Find the mean of the following set: (12, 15, 18, 20, 21)

$$\frac{12+15+18+20+21}{5} = \frac{86}{5} = 17.2$$

Absolute Deviation

Absolute deviation is a measure of how far a value in a set is from the mean of the set. For example, in the set used in the example for mean above, the mean was 17.2. The absolute deviation of each term in the set is the distance from that term to 17.2. So the absolute deviation of 12 is 5.2; the absolute deviation of 15 is 2.2; the absolute deviation of 18 is 0.8; etc.

Median

The median of a set of numbers is the number that is in the middle of the set when they are arranged in numerical order. If there are an even number of digits, the median is found by taking the average of the two numbers that are in the center (add them and divide by 2).

Example 1: *Find the median of the following set: (34, 25, 82, 11, 47)*

> In order, the set would read 11, 25, 34, 47, 82.

> The number in the middle (the median) is 34.

Example 2: *Find the median of the following set: (47, 23, 24, 89, 23, 43)*

> In order, the set would read 23, 23, 24, 43, 47, 89.

> In the middle are 24 and 43. Take their average to find the median.

$$\frac{24+43}{2} = \frac{67}{2} = 33.5$$

Mode

The mode is the number in a set that appears the most frequently. A set can have one mode, more than one mode, or no mode.

Example: *Find the mode of the following set: (34, 52, 34, 58, 31, 19)*

> The number that appears most frequently is 34. 34 is the mode.

Range

The **range** of a set describes the span between the numbers. The range is calculated by subtracting the lowest value in the set from the highest.

Example: *Find the range of the following set: (2, 59, 27)*

        The highest number in the set is 59. The lowest number is 2.

        59 – 2 = 57

        The range is 57.

Frequency Distribution

Frequency distribution is a representation of how many times the same event or piece of data occurs. Frequency distribution is often displayed in a table.

Example: *The scores on a recent math test were 100, 98, 95, 98, 86, 84, 80, 84, 75, 68, 80, 84, and 77. Create a table to show the frequency distribution of the scores.*

Score	Frequency
100	1
98	2
95	1
86	1
84	3
80	2
77	1
75	1
68	1

Probability

Probability is the likelihood of an event occurring. Probability is expressed as a quantifiable relationship between favorable outcomes and possible outcomes. It can be written as a ratio, fraction, decimal, or percent.

A **favorable outcome** is an event someone wants to happen. **Possible outcomes** are all of the events that could happen in a given situation.

Simple probability (P) is the ratio of favorable outcomes (O_f) to possible outcomes (O_p).

$$P_{\text{event}} = \frac{O_f}{O_p}$$

Example 1: *What is the probability of a coin toss landing on heads?*

When flipping a coin, there are two possible outcomes—heads or tails. The probability of getting heads is 1/2.

Example 2: *What is the probability of rolling a 5 on a die?*

When rolling a standard six-sided die, there are six possible outcomes. Rolling a 5 (the favorable outcome) is one of those possibilities. The probability of rolling a 5 is therefore 1/6.

Example 3: *Using a spinner with equal segments numbered 1-10, what is the probability of a spin landing on an even number?*

In this case, there are ten possible outcomes—landing on each of the ten segments. The favorable outcome is landing on an even number. In the set of numbers 1-10, there are five even numbers (2, 4, 6, 8, and 10). Any one of these would be a favorable outcome. The probability of landing on a even number is therefore 5/10, which reduces to 1/2.

The Fundamental Counting Principle

The **fundamental counting principle** states that if there are *m* ways to for one thing to happen and *n* ways for another thing to happen, then there are *m* x *n* ways for both to happen.

Example:
If you have 5 shirts and 3 pairs of pants, how many different outfits could you make?

5 x 3 = 15 outfits

These types of problems can also be solved using a visual aid called a **tree diagram**. A tree diagram lists all of the possible combinations of two events. The tree diagram for the example scenario above would look like this:

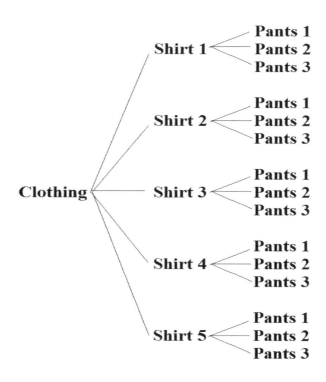

Counting all of the right-most possibilities (those farthest from the "trunk" of the tree) gives the total number of possibilities. In this case, the total is twelve possible outcomes.

Combinations

A **combination** involves choosing items (*r*) out of a group (*n*) in a situation where the order does not matter and there is no repetition.

The formula for a combination is:

$$_nC_r = \frac{n!}{(n-r)!\,r!}$$

This formula involves the use of **factorials**, represented by the exclamation point (!). A factorial is the product of a number and all of the counting numbers below it.

For example, 4! = 4 x 3 x 2 x 1 = 24

Example: *How many different groups of 3 students can be made from a class of 21?*

$$_nC_r = \frac{n!}{(n-r)!r!}$$

$$_{21}C_3 = \frac{21!}{(21-3)!3!}$$

$$_{21}C_3 = \frac{51090942171709440000}{18!3!}$$

$$_{21}C_3 = \frac{51090942171709440000}{(16402373705728000)(6)}$$

$$_{21}C_3 = \frac{51090942171709440000}{38414242234368000}$$

$$_{21}C_3 = 1,330$$

There are 1,330 possible groups.

Permutations

Permutations involve selecting items (r) out of a group (n) wherein the order *does* matter and there is no repetition. These problems involve arranging items in a certain order.

The formula for a permutation is:

$$_nP_r = \frac{n!}{(n-r)!}$$

Example: *How many different three-digit numbers can be made using only the digits 1, 3, 5, and 7?*

There are 4 digits to choose from and 3 are being selected.

$$_nP_r = \frac{n!}{(n-r)!}$$

$_4P_3 = \dfrac{4!}{(4-3)!}$

$_4P_3 = \dfrac{24}{1}$

$_4P_3 = 24$

There are 24 possible three-digit numbers.

Geometry

Geometry is the branch of mathematics concerned with the study of points, lines, shapes, and space. At the elementary level, students learn basic geometric concepts and properties, and how to use geometric concepts to solve mathematical and real-world problems.

Topics Addressed:

1. Geometric Figures

2. Solving Problems with Geometric Figures

3. Coordinate Geometry

Points

A point is an exact location on a plane surface.

. P

On a coordinate plane, a point is identified by a set of coordinates, giving the x and y values of the point's location on the coordinate plane.

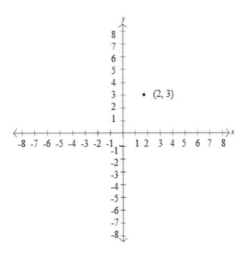

Lines, Line Segments, and Rays

A line is an object that is straight, thin, and infinitely long. It has arrows on both ends to show that it goes on forever in both directions.

l

Two special types of lines are parallel lines and perpendicular lines. Parallel lines are always equally spaced so that they never intersect each other.

Perpendicular lines intersect at a 90º angle.

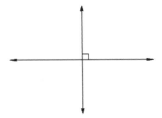

A **line segment** is a portion of a line that has two endpoints, which give it a definite length.

A **ray** has only one endpoint and is infinite in the other direction.

Angles

An **angle** is the space formed by two rays that meet at a common endpoint. Angles are measured in degrees.

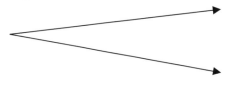

Angle Type	Definition	Example
Acute	The angle measures less than 90º	
Right	The angle measures exactly 90º	
Obtuse	The angle measures between 90º and 180º	
Straight	The angle measures exactly 180º	
Reflex	The angle measures greater than 180º	

Angles can also be described by their relationships to one another.

Complimentary angles are those whose measures add up to 90º.

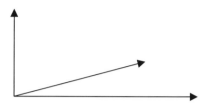

Supplementary angles are those whose measures add up to 180º.

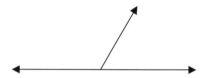

Two-Dimensional Shapes

A two-dimensional closed figure can be classified either as a polygon or a non-polygon. A **polygon** is a closed two-dimensional figure whose sides are all straight, non-overlapping line segments. A polygon is said to be **regular** if all of its sides and angles are equal and irregular if they are not. **Non-polygons** do not have sides that are all straight line segments and include such shapes as ellipses and circles. Polygons can be classified by the number of sides they have.

Name	Number of Sides
Triangle	3
Quadrilateral	4
Pentagon	5
Hexagon	6
Heptagon	7
Octagon	8
Nonagon	9
Decagon	10

Some of these categories of polygons can also be further broken down into subcategories. The most common ones elementary students will encounter are triangles and quadrilaterals. Triangles can be classified either by the types of angles they have or the length of their sides.

Triangles Classified by Angles		
Type of Triangles	Description	Example
Acute	All three angles are acute (measure less than 90º)	
Right	One angle is right (measures exactly 90º)	
Obtuse	One angle is obtuse (measures between 90º and 180º)	

Triangles Classified by Sides		
Type of Triangles	Description	Example
Equilateral	All three sides are equal in length	
Isosceles	Two sides are equal in length	
Scalene	No sides are equal in length	

Quadrilaterals can be divided into several subcategories based on characteristics such as angles, parallelism, and side length.

Quadrilateral- *four sides*	
Trapezoid- *one pair of parallel sides*	Parallelogram- *two pairs of equal parallel sides*

Rectangle- *four right angles*	Rhombus-- *four equal sides*

Square - *four right angles and four equal sides*

Three-Dimensional Shapes

A three-dimensional shape is a solid figure. Three-dimensional shapes are classified by their faces (the shape of each side and how many there are), their edges (where two face meet), and their vertices (points). There are several categories of solid figures, some of which are listed in the following chart:

Shape	Description	Example
Sphere	Round three-dimensional figure, like a ball	
Pyramid	Triangular of square base, with all other sides triangular that come together at a single point	
Rectangular prism	Six rectangular faces	
Cylinder	Two circular bases	
Cone	One circular base	
Cube	Six square faces	

Geometric Models and Nets

A **geometric model** can be constructed to show the shape of an object in geometric terms.

Geometric nets are two-dimensional figures that represent the faces of a three-dimensional shape. It's as if the three-dimensional figure has been cut apart along the edges and made to lay flat. Only certain three-dimensional figures can be made into geometric nets. Two of the most common examples are cubes and tetrahedrons (pyramids with a triangular base).

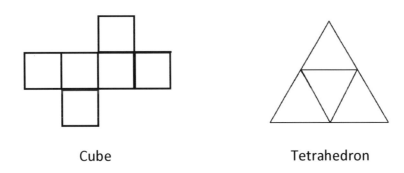

Cube   Tetrahedron

Measurements of Two-Dimensional Figures

The measure of the distance around a polygon is called the **perimeter**. The perimeter is found by adding up the lengths of all of the sides of a figure.

The distance around the outside of a circle is called the **circumference.** The circumference is found with the formula $C = \pi d$ or $C = 2\pi r$ where r is the radius and d is the diameter.

The measure of the space inside a two-dimensional figure is called the **area**.

Common Area Formulas	
Triangle	$A = \frac{1}{2}bh$
Parallelogram	$A = bh$
Rectangle	$A = lw$
Square	$A = s^2$
Circle	$A = \pi r^2$

Measurements of Three-Dimensional Figures

The measure of the **surface area** of a prism is found by adding up the areas of each of the faces. The measure of the space inside a three-dimensional object (its capacity) is called **volume**.

- Volume of a prism:

  $V = bh$ where b is the area of the base of the prism

- Volume of a pyramid or cone:

  $V = \frac{1}{3}bh$ where b is the area of the base of the object

- Volume of a sphere:

  $V = \frac{4}{3}\pi r^3$

Comparing Geometric Figures

Geometric figures can be compared using congruence and similarity.

Two figures are said to be **congruent** if they are exactly the same shape and size. The figures may be rotated, but the size and shape remain the same.

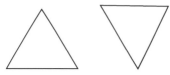

Two figures are said to be **similar** if they are the same shape (having the same angles and proportions) but different sizes.

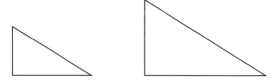

Symmetry

Symmetry creates a mirror image. A line of symmetry that passes through a shape divides the shape into two congruent halves such that the pieces are mirror images of one another. A shape can have no, one, or multiple lines of symmetry.

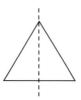

Transformations

Transformations are a way of manipulating geometric figures by changing their positions on a coordinate plane. There are three basic types of transformations, shown in the chart on the following page.

Name of Transformation	Description	Example
Reflection (Flip)	The transformed shape is a mirror image of the original	
Rotation (Turn)	The shape is turned on a point	
Translation (Slide)	The shape is shifted to another area on the plane but maintains its original orientation	

Coordinate graphing is a visual method of showing the relationships between numbers. Points, lines, geometric figures, equations, inequalities, and functions can all be represented using a coordinate graphing system.

The graphing space is called a **coordinate plane**. It consists of a grid created by a horizontal (x) axis and a vertical (y) axis.

The point where the two axes intersect is called the origin and has coordinates of (0,0). Every other point on the plane is given **coordinates** (locations) based on its distance from the origin. A point's location in reference to the x-axis is its x-coordinate and its location in reference to the y-axis is its y-coordinate. Coordinates are always listed in parenthesis in the format (x,y) and are called an **ordered pair**.

The graph below shows how points are given coordinates and located on a coordinate plane.

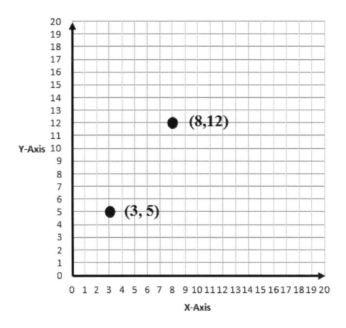

Coordinate grids can show both positive and negative values. Since the axes extend infinitely in each direction, any pair of numbers can be graphed. When the axes are extended in all directions, it creates a grid with four quadrants. The most commonly used quadrant is the first quadrant as seen above. The four quadrants together look like this:

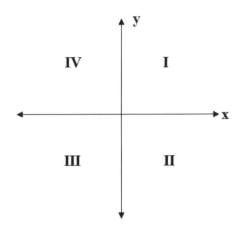

Points located in these quadrants have positive or negative coordinate values as follows:

- Quadrant I: (positive, positive)
- Quadrant II: (positive, negative)
- Quadrant III: (negative, negative)
- Quadrant IV: (negative, positive)

Coordinate planes are also commonly used to graph lines and other equations. See "Linear Functions and Equations" for the equations used to graph lines and to find slopes on a coordinate plane.

Linear Functions and Equations

A **linear function** is one whose graph is a straight line.

The equation of a line is commonly written in what is called **slope-intercept form**: **y = mx + b,** where x and y are the coordinates of any point on the line, m is the slope of the line, and b is the y-intercept (the value of y where the line crosses the y-axis.

The slope of a line can be found using any two points on the line with the **slope formula:** $m = \dfrac{y_2 - y_1}{x_2 - x_1}$

Example: Find the equation of the line shown on the graph below.

To generate the equation of the line, you need to know the slope *(m)* and the y- intercept *(b)*. The y-intercept in this case is 2, since the line crosses the y-axis at (0,2).

Use the slope formula to find the slope of the line:

$$m = \frac{y_2 - y_1}{x_2 - x_1} = \frac{-3-5}{4-(-4)} = \frac{-8}{8} = -1$$

Insert these values into the slope-intercept form to get the equation of the line.

y = *mx* + *b*

y = -x + 2

Science

Scientific knowledge is an essential part of students' academic foundation for life. Students develop skills in critical thinking, problem solving, and scientific methodology while learning about natural, physical, and chemical processes.

Test Structure

The Science section makes up 30% of Subtest II. Within Science, there are four major subcategories with which you must be familiar:

A. Characteristics of Science

B. Earth Science

C. Physical Science

D. Life Science

Each subcategory is divided into topics, which include the skills you must be able to demonstrate on the exam.

Characteristics of Science

This section covers how and why scientific inquiry is conducted, the skills and processes of scientific investigation, and the impact of science and technology on society and the environment.

Topics Addressed:

1. Skills for Scientific Inquiry
2. The Process of Scientific Inquiry
3. Science, Technology, and the Environment

The Nature and Goals of Science

Science is the study of the natural world through observation and experimentation. There are many reasons that people undertake scientific inquiry. Two of the major motivations for scientific exploration are:

- Desire to satisfy curiosity about the world

- Seeking practical applications of science that will benefit humanity

There are certain traits that scientists in any field tend to have in common that relate to the way they think about the world and about their work. Scientific thinking tends to involve:

- A natural curiosity about how things work

- Openness to new ideas

- An appropriate amount of skepticism and the refusal to take things at face value without investigation

- Willingness to work in cooperation with others

The Dynamic Nature of Science

Science is a field that is constantly changing as humans learn more and more about the world. Things that were considered the "truth" 1,000 or even 10 years ago may no longer hold true as new information comes to light. Scientific knowledge is constantly being revised as new theories are tested, as scientists build upon the work of their predecessors, and as technology allows for experimentation methods that were previously unavailable.

Some components of the dynamic nature of science include:

- **Durability**- the ability of something to stand the test of time

- **Tentativeness**- the idea that something has been made or done on a trial basis or as an experiment, or is not final or conclusive

- **Reliance on evidence**- Scientists must rely on evidence to back up their claims. They must also be willing to adjust previously held notions when new evidence comes to light.

- **Replication**- the idea that a valid experiment must have reproducibility and that when attempted again, the experiment would yield the same conclusions; replication is important for new scientific findings to be accepted

Integrated Process Skills

The study of science involved integrated process skills that are important to anyone working in the fields of science and engineering. These skills include:

- Observing
- Classifying
- Hypothesizing/making predictions
- Designing and conducting experiments
- Developing and using models
- Explaining their work to others

Science is the process by which we gain new knowledge of how the world works. The process is one of inquiry, wherein people ask questions about the world and make observations and perform experiments in order to find the answers to those questions.

Scientific Investigations

Scientific investigations can come in many forms, but the three major types are experiments, observations, and surveys.

- An **experiment** is a test performed under controlled conditions. Experiments can be conducted to test a hypothesis, to demonstrate something already known, or to try something new.

- **Observation** is watching an event very meticulously and keeping an account of what you see.

- A **survey** is used to gather information from a sampling of people by asking them all the same set of questions.

The Scientific Method

The main process used in scientific inquiry is known as the Scientific Method. This lays out the proper steps for scientific investigations.

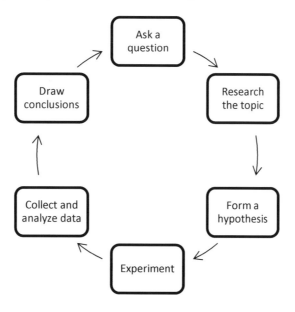

Collecting and Measuring Data

The methods used to collect data are very important in science. For scientific research to be considered reputable, the methods used to obtain the results must be reported along with the result and must be found to be honest and thorough.

Some important components of data collection include:

- Identifying and controlling variables

- Careful observation

- The accurate recording of measurement data using appropriate tools

Scientific Tools

There are many tools in science that students may learn about or use in experiments as they collect data.

- **Accelerometer-** used to measure the acceleration of moving objects

- **Balance-** used for measuring weight or mass

- **Barometer-** measures atmospheric pressure; used in weather studies

- **Bunsen burner-** open-flame heat source

- **Graduated cylinder-** container used for measuring liquid volume

- **Hot plate-** electric warming surface

- **Magnifier-** used to see things that cannot be seen with the naked eye

- **Microscope-** used for viewing things too small to be viewed with the naked eye or a regular magnifier

- **Petri dish-** small, round, plastic container used to grow bacteria, mold, etc.

- **Protractor-** used for measuring angles

- **Scale-** device used for measuring weight

- **Spectrometer-** an instrument used to measure the properties of light over a specific part of the spectrum

- **Telescope-** used to view objects in space

- **Thermometer or temperature probe-** measures heat

Analyzing and Representing Data

Once data has been collected from an experiment, a scientist needs a way to show that data and then analyze it and allow it to be analyzed by others. Data representation can take many forms depending on the experiment, but may include graphs, tables, charts, and/or narration.

Analysis of the data involves looking for patterns, checking the data against the hypothesis behind the experiment, and drawing logical conclusions. In some cases, the original hypothesis may be revised and become the subject of further experimentation.

Science, Technology, and the Environment

Science is a process shared by all humanity as they try to gain knowledge of the world. It has many connections to technology and society as a whole. Students should be encouraged to make these connections as cross-curricular and real-world connections to content make learning more meaningful.

Science and technology go hand in hand. Science is responsible for the vast array of technology we now enjoy. That advanced technology, in turn, allows science to continue and advance itself as it allows observation of phenomena and methods of experimentation never before possible.

The impact of science on the environment can be both positive and negative. Scientific progress has led to industrialization and a rapid increase in the amount of natural resources used. This has had harmful effects on the natural environment. Today, however, many scientists are working to create and improve new technologies that will allow people to use the Earth's resources more responsibly. This includes harnessing clean energy sources such as wind and solar power.

Science has far-reaching implications for society as it shapes how we understand the world and creates the technology we use on a daily basis. Careers in science are plentiful and include a wide variety of areas, including medicine, engineering, environmental science, astronomy, geology, computer science, science education, meteorology, biochemistry, and so many more. Students should be introduced to practical applications and careers in science in order to maintain a real world connection with the content they are learning.

Earth Science

Earth science is the study of the Earth, its composition, its history, its place in the universe, and its natural processes.

Topics Addressed:

1. The Structure and Processes of the Earth
2. Atmosphere, Climate, and Weather
3. The Earth in the Universe

The Structure of the Earth

Layers of the Earth

The Earth is composed of layers, each different in its composition.

- **Inner core**- the spherical solid center of the Earth, composed largely of iron and nickel; about 700-800 miles in diameter

- **Outer core**- a layer of liquid iron and nickel about 1,400 miles thick

- **Mantle**- a layer of hot, semi-solid rock about 1,800 miles thick that has currents, causing the plates of crust on top of it to move

- **Crust**- a series of solid plates that cover the Earth's surface, ranging from 5 to 30 miles thick

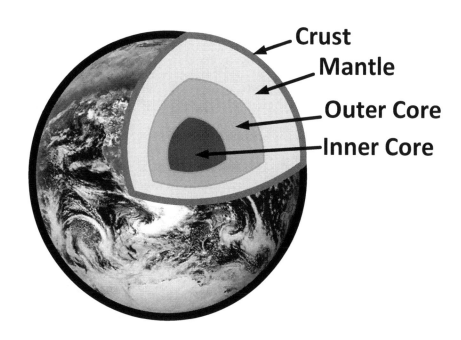

Plate Tectonics

The crust consists of continental (land) plates and oceanic plates. These plates are constantly shifted atop the mantle. The movement of these plates is known as **plate tectonics.**

The boundaries between plates help to shape the Earth's surface and can cause geological events. There are three ways plates can interact at their boundaries:

Type of Boundary	Example	Results
Convergent (colliding)	→ ←	Mountains, ridges, volcanoes
Divergent (separating)	← →	Bodies of water, new crust
Transform (rubbing)	↑ ↓	Earthquakes

The Earth's History

Geological history is the study of how Earth has developed over time. Over the course of its history, the Earth's landforms and life forms have undergone a great deal of change.

The **geologic record** helps scientists to learn about different parts of the Earth's history by examining layers of rock. Scientists base their findings on the law of superposition, which says that the oldest rocks are found at the bottom and newer rocks are found at the top. This helps scientists to date events and create a timeline of Earth's history.

Paleontology is the study of fossils. These scientists can study the origins and history of life by looking at the fossils contained within the layers of rock that compose the Earth.

The Processes of the Earth System

The Earth operates according to several systems and processes, all of which are interrelated and work together to create an environment in which life is sustainable.

The Earth's Position

The **tilt** of the Earth on its axis determines the amount of direct radiation from the sun at any given point on Earth. Locations closest to the equator receive the most direct solar rays and are therefore warmer throughout the year than the poles.

The **rotation** of the Earth is responsible for night and day and the gain and loss of heat and sunlight that accompany those times of day.

The **revolution** of the Earth around the sun is responsible for the changing of the seasons.

Heat

Heat is a process that greatly affects everything else on Earth. The Earth's heat comes from:

- Radioactivity at the Earth's core, which is responsible for the movement of plates and thus the creation of landforms.

- Solar energy, which heats Earth's surface.

Geological Processes

Geological processes are processes at work on the Earth's landforms. There are three major types of rocks, shown in the following chart:

Type of Rock	Description	Examples
Igneous	Formed through the cooling of magma	Granite, obsidian, pumice
Sedimentary	Formed when sediments (bits of eroded rock, sand, shells, fossils, etc.) are compressed into hard layers over time	Sandstone, limestone, shale
Metamorphic	Formerly igneous and sedimentary rocks that have morphed due to heat and pressure	Marble, quartzite, slate

These rock layers that make up the Earth's surface can change over time through forces such as weathering and erosion. **Weathering** is the breaking down of rock via environmental forces.

- Physical weathering occurs due to interaction with natural physical forces such as water, ice, and wind.

- Chemical weathering occurs due to exposure to chemicals, such as acid rain breaking down rock or oxygen in the air causing oxidation of a surface.

Erosion is when pieces of the weathered material are carried away via wind and water. Over time, these changes can have dramatic effects on the landscape, such as when a river erodes a plateau and forms a canyon.

One result of the breakdown of rock is the formation of soil. **Soil** is the loose material that sits on top of the rock on the Earth's surface. It is the substance in which many of Earth's plants grow. Its formation is the result of the physical and chemical breakdown of rock over time. In addition to rock, soil also contains dissolved minerals and organic material from decomposed plants and animals.

The **rock cycle** describes how rocks are created, changed, and destroyed.

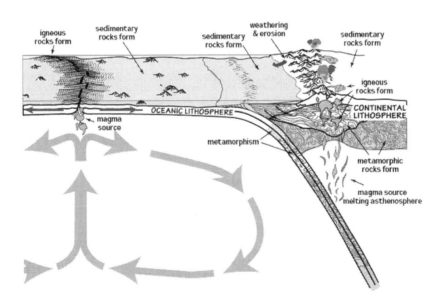

Water Cycle

The **water cycle** shows how water circulates through the Earth's surface and atmosphere.

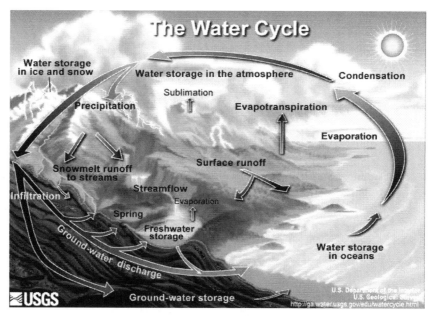

Layers of the Atmosphere

The atmosphere (the air above Earth) also exists in layers.

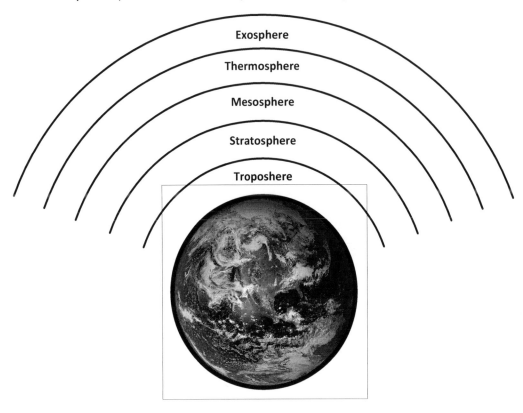

Exosphere

Thermosphere

Mesosphere

Stratosphere

Troposhere

Climates

Climates are long-term weather patterns for a particular area. The primary climates on Earth are:

- Tropical- hot and wet year-round

- Dry- temperature varies widely from day to night; very little precipitation

- Temperate- warm and wet in the summer, cool and dry in the winter

- Continental- found on large land masses, this climate has fairly low precipitation and temperatures can vary widely

- Polar- very cold; permanently frozen ground

Weather

Weather is the state of the atmosphere at a particular time and place, including temperature, air movement, precipitation, and humidity. The water cycle plays an enormous role in the weather, as it creates precipitation.

Clouds are the source of precipitation, as they are formed from accumulated moisture in the air. There are several major types of clouds:

Cloud Type	Description
Stratus	Horizontal layered clouds formed when warm, moist air passes over cool air
Cumulus	Large, puffy white clouds formed when warm, moist air is forced upward
Cirrus	Wispy clouds containing ice crystals that form at high altitudes
Nimbus	Clouds that produce precipitation

Air masses are large bodies of air that are fairly uniform as far as temperature, pressure, and moisture levels. Air masses have a significant impact on the weather. There are five major types of air masses that affect the weather in North America:

- Continental Arctic- originate in the Arctic and bring extremely cold temperatures

- Continental Polar- form just south of the Arctic Circle and create cold, dry conditions

- Maritime Polar- form over the northern parts of the Atlantic and Pacific Oceans and bring cool, moist weather

- Maritime Tropical- form over the southern part of the Atlantic and the Gulf of Mexico and bring warm temperatures and moisture

- Continental Tropical- forms over the desert in the southwestern United States and creates warm, dry weather

The weather in a particular area is greatly influenced by the season. Seasons are the four phases of the year caused by the Earth's revolution around the sun, marked by differences in weather patterns. Depending on their location on Earth, some areas experience the four seasons very distinctly, while in other areas, the weather remains more consistent.

The Earth is just one among many bodies in the universe.

Galaxies

Galaxies are systems of stars. The Earth belongs to the Milky Way Galaxy.

Astronomers (scientists who study celestial bodies) keep track of stars by organizing them into constellations.

Solar Systems

Within galaxies are solar systems, which consist of planets and other bodies orbiting a star. Our solar system consists of eight planets that orbit around the sun in elliptical patterns—Mercury, Venus, Earth, Mars, Jupiter, Saturn, Uranus, and Neptune—as well as their moons, asteroids, and other celestial objects.

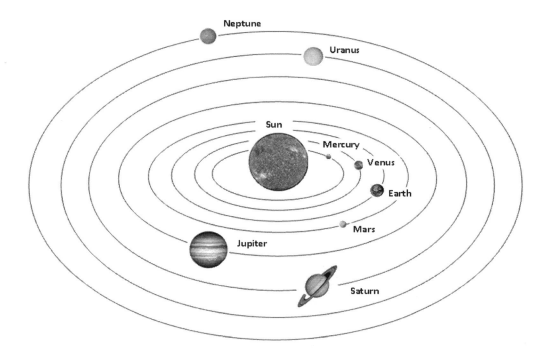

Moons

Moons revolve around planets, held in orbit by gravity. Some planets have more than one moon, but the Earth only has one, known as the Moon.

It takes the Moon 28 days to revolve around the Earth. The Moon does not give off any light of its own, but reflects light from the sun. Depending on the position of the Moon and the Earth in relationship to the sun, the Moon looks different from Earth at different times of the month. These are called the phases of the Moon.

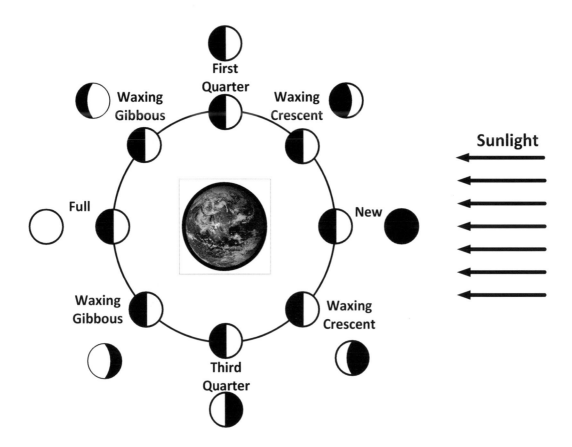

Eclipses are special events in which the sun, Moon, and Earth all line up in a direct path.

In a **solar eclipse**, the Moon is directly between the sun and the Earth and casts a shadow on the Earth's surface.

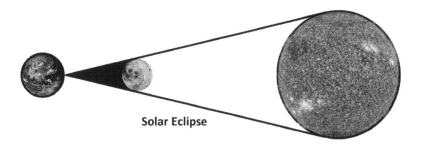

Solar Eclipse

In a **lunar eclipse**, the Earth is directly between the sun and the Moon, blocking light from hitting the Moon.

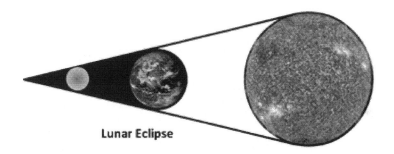

Lunar Eclipse

Other Celestial Objects

There are other objects in space besides stars, planets, and moons. Some of these include:

- **Asteroids**- large rocky objects in space; there is a large asteroid belt between Mars and Jupiter
- **Meteoroid**s- smaller rocky or metallic objects travelling through space
- **Meteorites**- meteoroids that enter Earth's atmosphere
- **Meteors**- streaks of light that trail behind meteorites as they burn in Earth's atmosphere
- **Comets**- icy bodies that form tails as they near the sun

Physical Science

Physical science is the study of the physical and chemical materials, processes, and forces that make up our environment.

Topics Addressed:

1. The Structure and Properties of Matter
2. Energy
3. Forces and Motion

The Atomic Structure of Matter

Matter is the physical substance of which everything is composed. Matter comes in many different varieties and can even change forms.

The most basic unit of matter is the **atom**. An atom is made up of a center cluster of positively charged **protons** and non-charged **neutrons** called a **nucleus**, as well as outer layers of negatively charged **electrons.**

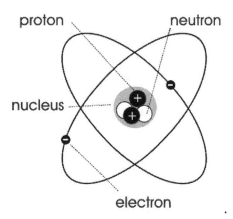

An **element** is a type of substance that cannot be broken down into different types of matter. Currently there are 114 known elements and they are listed by atomic number in the **periodic table**.

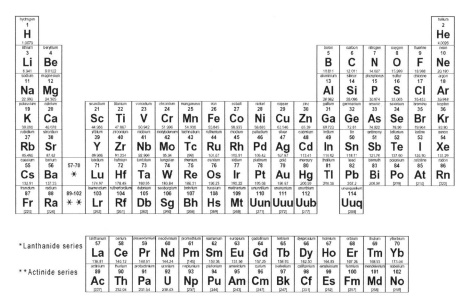

How Elements Combine

Elements combine in different ways to make up all matter. Two or more atoms combined into an electrically neutral structure are called a **molecule**. Molecules can contain atoms that are of the same element or of different elements.

A **compound** is the chemical bonding of two or more different elements.

Mixtures occur when two unlike substances are mixed together without a chemical reaction. Mixtures can be **homogeneous** (if they are the same throughout) or **heterogeneous** (if the components are not distributed uniformly).

Solutions occur when one type of substance (called the **solute**) dissolves into another substance (called the **solvent**). Solutions are considered homogenous mixtures because the new substance is the same throughout as the solute is distributed evenly.

States of Matter

Matter can exist in three forms or states—solid, liquid, and gas.

- **Solids** have molecules that are relatively close together and have strong molecular forces that hold the substance into a fixed shape with a fixed volume.

- **Liquids** have weaker molecular forces than solids, which allow them to move fluidly and take on the shape of their container, while still maintaining a fixed volume.

- **Gases** have weak molecular bonds which allow the molecules to move rapidly. Gases take on both the shape and volume of their containers, as they will spread out as far as their container will allow.

Matter can change its state through changes in temperature and pressure. These changes are called **phases changes**.

From	To	Name of Change
Solid	Liquid	Melting
Solid	Gas	Sublimation
Liquid	Gas	Vaporization
Liquid	Solid	Freezing
Gas	Liquid	Condensation
Gas	Solid	Deposition

Properties of Matter

Matter can be described according to certain properties. These include:

- Mass- a measure of the amount of matter in an object

- Volume- the amount of space an object or substance takes up

- Points of phase change- the temperature at which a certain substance undergoes a phase change (i.e. boiling point, freezing point)

- Hardness- a measure of how resistant a subject is to physical change (e.g., scratching, indentation) when force is applied

- Texture- the tactile quality of a surface

Matter is also subject to certain physical laws. The **Law of Conservation of Matter** states that matter can be neither created nor destroyed, but it can be rearranged.

Physical and Chemical Changes

Changes in matter can be classified as either physical or chemical.

Physical changes affect the form of a substance but not its chemical composition. Some examples of physical changes are:

- Phases changes (boiling, melting, freezing, etc.)

- Tearing

- Crumpling

Chemical changes do involve an alteration of the chemical composition of a substance at the molecular level. Some examples of chemical changes are:

- Burning
- Rusting
- Cooking

Energy is defined as the ability to do work. Energy comes in several different forms, including kinetic, potential, thermal, radiant, electrical, mechanical, chemical, and nuclear. While energy cannot be created or destroyed (**Law of Conservation of Energy**) it can be transferred to another form.

Kinetic and Potential Energy

The two most basic states of energy are kinetic and potential. **Kinetic energy** is energy in motion. **Potential energy** is stored energy that can be converted to kinetic energy. An object in motion has kinetic energy, while an object at rest has potential energy.

Thermal Energy

Thermal energy (or **heat**) is the energy of a substance or system related to its temperature. Heat is caused by the vibration of molecules. The faster the vibration, the more heat will be produced.

Heat can be transferred in three major ways:

1. **Conduction**- heat transfer via a conductive material such as metal

2. **Convection**- heat transfer through the collision of liquid or gas molecules

3. **Radiation**- heat is transmitted without contact via infrared radiation

Radiant Energy

Radiant energy is the energy of electromagnetic waves such as light.

Electric Energy

Electric energy is a form of energy that is delivered or absorbed by an electrical circuit. An **electrical circuit** is the path along which an electrical current flows. There are two main types of circuits:

- **Series circuit**- circuit in which resistors are arranged in a chain so that the current only has only path to take

- **Parallel circuit**- resistors are arranged so that there are multiple paths for the current to pass through

Conductors are those materials that allow electrical current to flow through them, such as metals. **Insulators** are those materials that do not allow the flow of electrical currents, such as plastic and wood.

Mechanical Energy

Mechanical energy is related to the use of machines.

Chemical Energy

Chemical energy is the energy stored in the bonds between atoms in molecules. Chemical energy contains the potential for a **chemical reaction**, wherein one set of chemical substances is transformed into another.

Nuclear Energy

Nuclear energy results from a change in the nucleus of atoms. There are two types of nuclear reactions. When nuclei are split, this is called **fission**. Fission is the type of reaction used in creating atomic bombs and nuclear reactors. The joining of nuclei is called **fusion**, which occurs in the sun and in hydrogen bombs.

Interactions Between Energy and Matter

Energy can interact with matter in a variety of ways. This includes:

- **Electricity** moves through matter (specifically, a conductor) as a current. Electricity can produce light, heat, motion, and magnetic force. Electricity can be measured in terms of voltage and amperage. **Voltage** is a measure of the amount of force in an electrical current. **Amperage** measures the strength of an electrical current as it passes through a conductor.

- **Magnetism** involves the forces exerted by magnets on other magnets. All magnets have two poles (called "North" and "South") which have opposite charges. Opposite poles attract one another, while similar poles repel.

- **Sound** moves in waves caused by the vibrations of particles. The three major characteristics of sound are pitch, amplitude, and quality. Differences in **pitch** are cause by the rate of the vibrations. The faster the vibrations, the higher the pitch. **Amplitude** is how loud a sound is, which is caused by the force used to create the sound. The greater the force that created the sound, the louder the sound will be. Sound **quality** is also known as timbre and includes other characteristics that allow the ear to distinguish between sounds of the same pitch and amplitude.

Motion

Motion is change is an object's position. The fundamental principles of motion are those found in Newton's Laws of Motion. His three laws are:

1. An object in motion will stay in motion and an object at rest will stay at rest until acted upon by an outside force. (inertia)
2. An object will move in the direction of the force that was applied to it, with an acceleration proportional to the force applied. Force = mass x acceleration
3. For every action, there is an equal and opposite reaction.

Force

Force is an influence that causes an object to undergo a change in motion. There are different types:

Type	Definition
Applied Force	Force applied directly to an object by another object or person (e.g. pushing and pulling)
Gravity	The force with which a massively large object (such as the Earth or another planet or moon) pulls other, smaller objects toward itself ; gravity on Earth pulls everything toward the Earth's center
Friction	The force exerted by an object or surface as another object slides across it
Air Resistance	Force exerted upon objects as they move through the air
Normal Force	The support force applied when an object comes is in contact with another stable object
Tension Force	Force present in a cable when pulled on both ends
Spring Force	The force a spring exerts on any object attached to it
Electromagnetic Force	A natural force that affects electrically charged particles

When the result of all forces acting on an object is zero, the object is said to be in equilibrium and is either at rest or is in unaccelerated motion.

Simple Machines

The most basic types of machines are known as simple machines. These systems perform work with very few parts.

There are six basic types of simple machines:

Simple Machine	Description	Example
Incline Plane	Used to help move things up or down by reducing the force needed by increasing the distance	
Lever	Used to lift a load using applied force and a fulcrum or pivot	
Pulley	A system that uses a wheel and a rope to make it easier to lift things	
Screw	An inclined plane wrapped around a pole that can be used for holding objects together or for lifting	
Wedge	An object with at least one slanting side resulting in a very narrow edge, used to separate or cut things	
Wheel and Axle	Allows objects to move more quickly and easily by rolling them	

Life Science

Life science is the study of living things on Earth, including their characteristics, biological processes, behaviors, history, and relationships.

Topics Addressed:

1. Characteristics of Living Things

2. Life Cycles, Reproduction, and Heredity

3. Organisms and the Environment

In science anything that is or has ever been alive is considered a living thing. Anything that has never and never will be alive is considered a non-living thing.

Characteristics of Living Things

Living things share several common traits:

- Require nourishment
- Use energy
- Are capable of growth
- Reproduce
- Have definite life spans
- Respond and adapt to their environment
- Are made up of **cells**

Cells

Living things are made up of cells. The purposes of cells are to create energy for the organism, to create proteins, and to reproduce.

Cells are organized in the following manner:

- **Tissue**- a group of cells
- **Organ**- a group of tissues working together for a common purpose
- **Organ system**- a group of organs working together
- **Organism**- a complete living thing, made up of systems

Plant and Animal Cells

Plant cells and animal cells share many similarities but plant cells contain some parts that animal cells do not.

Parts of Plant and Animal Cells	
Part	**Function**
Nucleus	Control center of the cell which contains DNA
Cytoplasm	Everything outside the nucleus
Endoplasmic reticulum	Transport system for molecules between the nucleus and the cytoplasm
Ribosomes	Make proteins
Golgi bodies	Package and transport proteins
Mitochondria	Create energy (ATP)
Vacuoles	Store food and water
Lysosomes	The digestive system of the cell; holds enzymes that are used to break down molecules
Cell membrane	Permeable boundary of the cell that allows the passage of needed

Parts Only Found in Plant Cells	
Chloroplasts	Contain chlorophyll, used in food production (photosynthesis)
Cell wall	Rigid outer structure of the cell materials in and waste out
Cell membrane	Permeable boundary of the cell that allows the passage of needed

Animal cell:

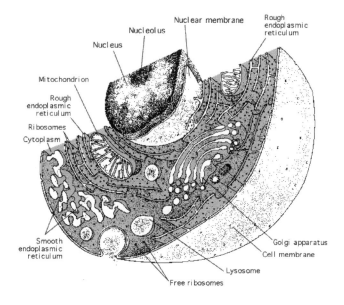

Plant cell:

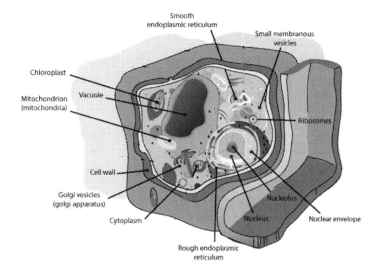

Structure of Plants

Part	Function
Roots	Hold the plant into the ground; absorb water and nutrients from the soil
Stem	Carry nutrients from the roots to the rest of the plant
Leaves	Make food for the plant through photosynthesis, a process by which the plant uses its chlorophyll, water, nutrients, carbon dioxide, and energy from the sun to make food and oxygen
Flower	Site of reproduction

Structure of Animals

Animals' organ systems provide the basic functions which enable them to live. While animals all possess some form of these systems, the organs they contain may differ among species. The chart below contains information about each system and provides the names of some of the human body parts for these systems.

System	Function
Digestive	Provides nutrition to the body
Circulatory	Carries blood throughout the body
Respiratory	Brings in oxygen and expels carbon dioxide
Excretory	Eliminates waste
Nervous	Carries electrical signals from brain to the cells
Reproductive	Creates offspring
Muscular and/or Skeletal	Provides structure and allows movement
Regulatory	Regulates body functions

Human Body Systems

The human body contains the following systems:

System	Function	Body Parts Involved
Digestive	Provides nutrition to the body	Mouth, tongue, esophagus, stomach, large and small intestines
Circulatory	Carries blood throughout the body	Heart, veins, arteries
Respiratory	Brings in oxygen and expels carbon dioxide	Nose, mouth, trachea, lungs
Excretory	Eliminates waste	Skin, kidneys, bladder
Nervous	Carries electrical signals from brain to the cells	Brain, nerves
Reproductive	Creates offspring	Uterus, ovaries, testes, penis
Muscular	Allows movement	Muscles
Skeletal	Provides structure and allows movement	Bones
Endocrine	Regulates body functions through hormones	Brain, glands throughout the body, pancreas
Immune	Defends the body from illness	T-cells carried by blood
Lymphatic	Removes excess fluid from around cells; eliminates bacteria	Lymph nodes
Integumentary	Protects the body against the environment	Skin, hair, nails

Life Cycles

One of the characteristics of a living thing is that it has a finite life span. Every organism goes through a life cycle, made up of the various stages that are common to all living things:

1. The organism comes into existence

2. Growth

3. Metamorphosis

4. Maturation

5. Reproduction

6. Death

Reproduction and Heredity

Reproduction is the creation of new organisms of the same species. Reproduction is essential for the continuation of the species. **DNA** (deoxyribonucleic acid) contains the codes for proteins, which are the building blocks of life. DNA is made up of two strands that contain **genes** that dictate traits for an organism. Groups of genes make up **chromosomes**.

Organisms reproduce using one of two types of reproduction:

1. **Asexual reproduction**- New cells are created from only one parent organism via cells that produce two identical sets of chromosomes and then split to form new cells.

2. **Sexual reproduction**- Reproduction involves two parent organisms, each of whom contribute a reproductive cell containing one set of chromosomes. The two combine to create cells with a full set of chromosomes.

Chromosomes come in pairs and each half of the pair comes with genes for each trait. The combination of these genes determine the organism's traits. Traits can be classified as either **dominant** or **recessive**.

Dominant genes are more likely to appear in an organism. Recessive genes will generally be hidden by dominant genes if dominant genes are also present.

If there are two dominant genes, the dominant trait will appear in the organism. If there is one dominant and one recessive gene, the dominant trait will appear in the organism. If both genes are recessive, the recessive trait will appear in the organism.

For example, brown eyes are a trait that is dominant over blue eyes. If each parent contributes genes for both brown (B) and blue (b) eyes, the possibilities for the child will be:

	B	b
B	BB	Bb
b	Bb	bb

If even one dominant trait (B) is present in a pair, it will appear in the organism, therefore, in three out of the four possible combinations of genes for this child (75%), the child will have brown eyes.

Organisms and the Environment

Organisms all share space on the Earth and must therefore live in cooperation in order to survive.

The **biosphere** is the environment on Earth in which living things exist. It includes the land, the water, and the air.

Within the biosphere are smaller environments, known as ecosystems. An **ecosystem** is a community of organisms and their physical environment. An ecosystem requires an energy source (such as the sun), a means to convert that energy to glucose (plant life), and a means of recycling organic materials.

Ecosystems operate and transfer energy according to a cycle:

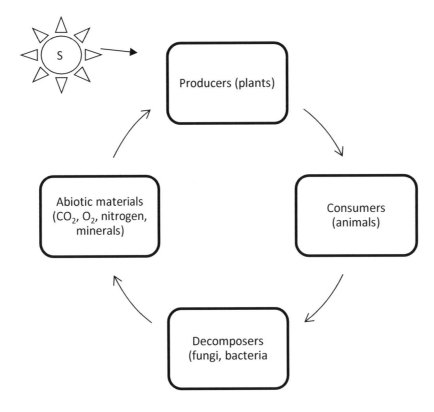

The Food Chain

The way that energy moves through living things in an ecosystem is through the **food chain**. The food chain describes the order in which animals consume plants and other animals.

Plants create energy in the form of ATP through photosynthesis. They are known as **producers**. To get this energy for themselves, animals must either eat those plants (herbivores) or eat another animal (carnivore), which somewhere down the line has eaten a plant and gotten its energy.

Animals are known as **consumers** because they consume (eat) other organisms. Those who eat plants are known as primary consumers. Those who eat primary consumers are known as secondary consumers, etc. At the highest level of a food chain are those top consumers who have few natural predators and are therefore unlikely to be eaten.

Here is an example of a food chain in an ecosystem:

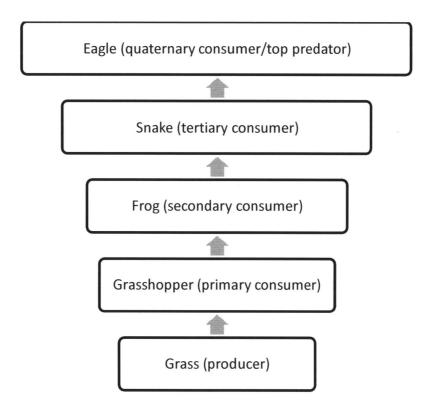

Disruptions to Ecosystems

The balance of ecosystems is delicate and can be disrupted by many causes that include:

- Interruptions in the food chain

- Depletion of any species

- Natural disasters

- Change in energy supply

- Human causes, such as pollution, deforestation, depletion of resources, mining, and radiation

Health Education, Physical Education, and the Arts

Health, Physical Education, and the Arts are important components of a well-rounded education and help students to learn with both mind and body.

Test Structure

The Health Education, Physical Education, and the Arts section makes up 17% of Subtest II. Within this section, there are two major subcategories with which you must be familiar:

A. Health and Physical Education

B. The Arts

Each subcategory is divided into topics, which state the skills you must be able to demonstrate on the exam.

Health and Physical Education

Students will learn about the structures and processes of the human body along with how to take care of that body through nutrition, physical fitness, disease prevention, and making healthy life choices.

Topics Addressed:

1. Growth and Development
2. Promoting Healthy Lifestyles
3. Physical Fitness

Healthy education at the elementary level includes information about the growth and development of the human body. This includes such topics as:

- Growth
- Body parts and systems
- Puberty
- Reproduction and sexual health

Human Body Systems

The human body contains the following systems:

System	Function	Body Parts Involved
Digestive	Provides nutrition to the body	Mouth, tongue, esophagus, stomach, large and small intestines
Circulatory	Carries blood throughout the body	Heart, veins, arteries
Respiratory	Brings in oxygen and expels carbon dioxide	Nose, mouth, trachea, lungs
Excretory	Eliminates waste	Skin, kidneys, bladder
Nervous	Carries electrical signals from brain to the cells	Brain, nerves
Reproductive	Creates offspring	Uterus, ovaries, testes, penis
Muscular	Allows movement	Muscles
Skeletal	Provides structure and allows movement	Bones
Endocrine	Regulates body functions through hormones	Brain, glands throughout the body, pancreas
Immune	Defends the body from illness	T-cells carried by blood

Maintaining a healthy lifestyle involves more than just nutrition, exercise, or good hygiene alone. It's about making healthy choices every day that affect the whole body—physically, mentally, and emotionally.

Nutrition

Nutrition tells students how to eat in a way that is healthy. Food is required to provide energy that the body needs to carry on its functions. Eating healthy foods provides the body with the best possible energy. Three basic components of food are protein, carbohydrates, and fat.

- Proteins assist with muscle growth.
- Carbohydrates provide energy.
- Fat is stored for the body to use when it doesn't get enough food.

Foods come in five basic groups—grains, meats, dairy, fruits, and vegetables. (Sweets and other innutritious foods are considered empty calories and are not a part of these food groups.) A healthy diet includes a balance of these groups. Students should also be aware of some of the adverse effects of not maintaining a nutritious diet, including obesity, heart disease, and diabetes.

Disease Prevention

Communicable diseases are those illnesses that can be spread from person to person. Students should learn the important steps in communicable disease prevention. Personal hygiene, such as hand washing, covering the mouth when coughing or sneezing, and general cleanliness can help prevent the spread of communicable diseases. Some diseases are also prevented through the use of vaccinations, which help people develop a resistance to a disease by putting a small amount of an inactive virus into the person's body, allowing the immune system to create antibodies against it.

Non-communicable diseases are those illnesses that cannot be spread from person to person. Major non-communicable diseases include cancer, diabetes, and heart disease. The risks of many of these diseases are lessened through healthy lifestyle choices such as proper nutrition, exercise, and avoiding harmful substances.

Safety

Health education also involves teaching students proper safety. Students need to be aware of everyday hazards that can cause harm and be prepared for emergency situations. They need to know how to prevent harm and how to react when an incident does occur.

Major safety concepts at the elementary level include such topics as:

- Proper behavior in traffic (including pedestrian and bicycle etiquette and safety)
- Fire safety
- Household hazards
- Playground/outdoor safety
- Emergency procedures for school and home, including how to get help
- Basic first aid
- Stranger safety

Social, Mental, and Emotional Health

Students should be led to identify and express their feelings and learn to direct those feelings in appropriate ways.

Students must also learn appropriate ways to interact with others, including:

- Basic social skills and manners
- Negotiation skills
- Peer mediation
- Conflict resolution
- Refusal skills
- Handling peer pressure
- How to identify, prevent, and cope with bullying

Students should also be familiar with mental health risks such as depression and suicide, learn the warning signs, and learn how to respond.

Drugs and Alcohol

Drugs and alcohol are substances that can be harmful to the body. Even legal drugs like medicine can be harmful if used improperly. Students should understand the classification of medicinal drugs as prescription or over-the-counter and understand the risks of improper use of even these supposedly helpful substances. Students should be aware of the various types of drugs—both legal and illegal—and their potential effects on the body.

There are three basic categories of drugs—stimulants, depressants, and hallucinogens.

Type of Drug	Examples	Effects on the Body
Stimulants	Nicotine, caffeine, cocaine, amphetamines, ecstasy, meth	Elevated mood, high followed by a crash, paranoia, restlessness, irritability
Depressants	Alcohol, heroin, morphine, codeine, barbiturates, tranquilizers, marijuana	Depressed central nervous system, slow responses, reduced pain, reduced inhibitions
Hallucinogens	LSD, PCP, psilocybin	Altered mental perception, hallucinations

Physical fitness is the body's overall state of physical health—its ability to effectively function during both work and leisure activities. It involves muscle strength and endurance, cardiovascular endurance, flexibility, and body mass index.

Benefits of Physical Fitness

Promoting physical fitness at an early age increases the likelihood that the child will grow to remain active throughout his or her life. Physical fitness helps to prevent many diseases such as obesity, heart disease, and type ii diabetes. It can also improve mood and the body's overall ability to function and feel good on a day to day basis.

Physical fitness also has social benefits. Many physical activities are done with others and sports and other group activities promote cooperation, teamwork, healthy competition, self-esteem, communication, negotiation, trust, conflict resolution, and other important social skills.

Kinesthetic Development

Children grow and develop at different rates. Children of the same age should not all be expected to perform the same tasks at the same levels. Through play (both unstructured and structured), motor skills naturally develop. As children mature, so will their abilities and activities appropriate for their level will shift. At the early elementary levels, students will primarily need to develop body management, cardiovascular fitness, and large muscle skills. Over time, emphasis will shift to add more specific skills, muscle strength, and flexibility.

Motor Skills and Movement

There are several major types of physical skills that can be developed through physical activities.

- **Locomotor skills** are those skills that enable movement over distances. For children, these include such movements as walking, running, hopping, leaping, galloping, and skipping.

- **Non-locomotor skills** are movements that do not involve travel over distances. Common non-locomotor skills for children include balance, twisting, turning, bending, and stretching.

- **Manipulative skills** involve using an implement such as a ball or other piece of equipment. Common manipulative skills for children include catching, throwing, carrying, kicking, and dribbling.

- **Body management skills** require students to have the perceptual awareness and physical control necessary to be aware of the space around them and to control their physical movements within that space.

The Arts

This section covers the basic terms, techniques, and processes associated with the major forms of fine arts, as well as the importance of the arts to society.

Topics Addressed:

1. Dance
2. Music
3. Visual Arts
4. Theater Arts
5. The Arts as Expression and Communication
6. The Role of the Arts

Dance is a movement activity important to children as they learn physical coordination and rhythm.

Elements of Dance

The basic elements of dance are force, space, and time.

- **Force** is the use of energy while moving.
- **Space** is the area in which the dance movement occurs. There are several types of space involved in dance:
    - Shape- the way the body is positioned as it moves
    - Pathway- the patterns that the body makes as it moves
    - Level- the distance of the body from the ground
    - Direction- which way the body moves (up, down, left, right, forward, backwards)
- **Time:** The tempo and beat of the music and the duration of the dance.

Forms and Styles of Dance

There are many forms of dance, characterized by the types of movements used, the rhythms, the techniques, the footwear, and the music that accompanies the dance. Different cultural groups and period of history have also had their own forms of dance.

Some of the major forms of dance include:

- Ballet
- Jazz
- Tap
- Lyrical
- Modern
- Hip-hop
- Swing
- Latin
- Country-western
- Folk

Music is an important part of childhood education. It can be played for pleasure, but it also teaches important transferrable lessons in rhyme, rhythm, repetition, and patterns. There are cognitive, linguistic, social, emotional, and physical benefits to playing music.

Elements of Music

The basic elements of music are rhythm, melody, harmony, texture, and volume.

- **Rhythm** is the beat of the music—how music connects to time. The speed of a piece of music is known as the tempo. Children can connect with rhythm through clapping, snapping, or stamping their feet with the rhythm; through dance movements; or through playing rhythm instruments like drums or tambourines.

- **Melody** is the "tune" of a song. It is made up of different pitches caused by sound vibrations. Children can create melodies with their voices or with instruments.

- **Harmony** is created when more than one note is played at a time. Children can create harmony with their voices or with instruments.

- **Texture** is how many different lines of music occur at the same time. Children start out learning monophony—songs with a single line. Eventually, they may learn to participate in increasingly complex textures like rounds or songs where singers and instruments play different lines.

- **Volume** is how loud or soft music is. Children can experiment with volume in both vocal and instrumental music.

Musical Instruments

Most musical instruments fall into one of four basic categories—strings, woodwinds, brass, and percussion. These groups are known as "families" of instruments.

Strings are instruments whose sound is produced by plucking, striking, or bowing a (usually metal) string. Common string instruments include:

- Violin
- Viola
- Cello
- Bass
- Guitar
- Piano
- Banjo
- Mandolin
- Harp

Woodwinds are instruments whose sound is produced by blowing air into a reed or across an edge. Common woodwinds include:

- Clarinet
- Flute
- Piccolo
- Oboe
- Bassoon
- Recorder

Brass instruments are instruments made of metal whose sound is produced when a musicians blows air in a buzzing fashion into a mouthpiece, which causes the air inside the instrument to vibrate and make sound. Common brass instruments include:

- Trumpet
- Trombone
- Tuba
- French horn
- Bugle
- Cornet

Percussion instruments are varied in form but are used to create a rhythm for a piece of music. Different kinds of percussion instruments can be shaken, struck, or scratched to make different sounds. Common percussion instruments include:

- Drums
- Tambourine
- Cymbals
- Xylophone
- Marimbas
- Chimes
- Triangle
- Glockenspiel
- Maracas

The visual arts allow children to experiment with expression in a variety of mediums. Examples of visual arts appropriate for the elementary level are drawing, coloring, painting, sculpture, and collage.

Elements of Visual Arts

The basic elements of art are line, shape, color, texture, form, value, and space.

- **Line:** In art, a line is defined as a path made by a moving point, object, or mark. Unlike in math, a line doesn't have to be straight. It can be curved, squiggly, curly, straight, wavy, jagged, zigzag, dotted, dashed, smooth, or broken. Lines can go in any direction.

- **Shape:** A shape is a two-dimensional enclosed area. Shapes are not limited to traditional geometric shapes and may be organic or irregular.

- **Color:** Color is derived from absorbed or reflected light. The primary colors are red, blue, and yellow. Secondary colors, formed by blending primary colors, and green, purple, and orange. Students often learn about the colors through color mixing experiments and through the color wheel.

- **Texture:** Texture is the way something feels (if three-dimensional, called real texture) or looks like it would feel if you could touch it (if two-dimensional, called implied texture).

- **Form:** A form is a three-dimensional object—something with height, width, and depth.

- **Value :** Value refers to the darkness or lightness of an object. Value is created through light, shadow, shade, and tints. Shades are created by adding black to a color, while tints are created by adding white.

- **Space:** Space is emptiness either in or around an object. Positive space is the area that a shape takes up and negative space is the area around it. Objects that appear to be in the front of a piece of art are said to be in the foreground; those in the mid-space are in the middle ground; and those that appear farthest from the viewer are said to be in the background.

Materials and Processes

"Visual arts" is a broad and diverse category that includes many art forms, each of which requires its own set of materials and processes. The chart below gives example of some of the major forms of visual arts.

Visual Art Form	Description
Animation	Creating drawn, sculpted, or computer-generated art that appears to move, bringing it to life for film
Collage	Attaching overlapping paper materials to a surface
Design	Developing a plan for a new object; includes graphic design, fashion design, interior design, building design, etc.
Drawing	Representing objects or forms on a surface primarily using lines; usually done with pencil, crayon, charcoal, or ink
Film	A motion picture
Illustration	Creating pictures to accompany text
Mixed Media	Using a variety of materials and techniques within a single piece of art
Painting	Creating a picture by applying paint with a brush
Photography	Using a camera to take pictures
Printmaking	Creating prints, typically on paper; common techniques include woodcut, engraving, etching, screen-printing, and lithography
Sculpture	Creating a 3-dimensional form by carving and/or molding materials such as clay and stone

A drama is a story acted out for an audience. Drama can be used in the classroom for story-telling, role playing, reenactment, or interpretation.

Story

The story of a drama contains the same basic elements as any other literary story— introduction, setting, rising action, conflict, climax, falling action, and conclusion. A drama can be about almost any subject. Two common forms of drama are comedy and tragedy. Comedies are usually light-hearted and have a happy ending. Tragedies have an unhappy ending, usually involving the downfall of a main character.

In most dramas, the story is written first before it is performed. The written form is called a script. In some cases, actors perform all or some actions and words that are not scripted. This is called improvisation.

Characters

Characters are played by actors. Just like in other forms of narrative, there is usually a protagonist and an antagonist. Typically, a list of characters, which may or may not include brief descriptions, is given at the beginning of a script.

Dialogue

Dialogue is how stories are told through drama. Dialogue consists of the spoken words of the actors as their characters speak to one another. A monologue is one character speaking for an extended period of time while others are on stage. A soliloquy occurs when a character speaks with no one else present on stage.

Movement

In addition to dialogue, most scripts include stage directions that give the actors a basic idea of how to move on stage. This may be as simple as directions for entrances and exits, or may include much more detailed descriptions of how to move or how a line should be said.

Stage

The stage is the area used for performance. It may or may not be a raised area.

Sets and Costumes

Sometimes, sets and costumes are used to enhance dramas and make them more realistic for the audience. Sets are elements such as backdrops and furniture that help transform the stage space into the setting of the play. Costumes are the clothes, shoes, makeup, wigs, etc. that make the actors physically resemble their characters.

Dramatic Forms and Styles

Drama is a literary form in which the story is presented through dialogue and is meant to be performed for an audience. Common forms of drama intended for children include:

- Plays
- Skits
- Puppetry
- Story theater

There are several major dramatic forms. These are categories into which the stories and styles of most plays fit.

- Comedy- lighthearted and often funny; usually contains a happy ending for the protagonist
- Tragedy- contains an unhappy ending for the protagonist
- Drama- has a serious tone
- Melodrama- a piece in which everything is exaggerated and intended to appeal to the emotions
- Musical- a play in which singing plays an essential part
- Romance- a play focused on a romantic relationship
- Farce- an absurd comedy

The Arts as Expression and Communication

The arts can be used as a means of communication and self-expression. Thoughts and feelings that may be difficult to put into words can be brought out through the creative self-expression that the arts allow.

The arts encourage self-confidence, independence, and the use of strengths and talents. They help to develop children's imaginations and promote higher order thinking skills.

Connecting with the Arts

The arts can easily connect to one another, to other disciplines, and to students' everyday lives. Overall, the arts have been shown to improve higher order thinking skills, self-discipline, physical skills, communication skills, concentration, memory, and cooperation.

Integrating the arts into other subjects increases success in those areas. Some examples of how to integrate the arts into other areas are:

- Music- create a song to help students remember a concept in any subject area, use music to teach rhyme, use period music to enhance understanding of historical settings
- Dance- create motions to help students remember steps or a concept in any subject, learn the dance of a particular culture or time period
- Drama- act out scenes from literary works, situations from math or science word problems, or historical events; role play; use drama to reinforce social skills
- Visual Arts- use drawings to accompany journaling; illustrate literary works, scientific processes, or historical events

Practice Examination
Subtest I

Reading and Language Arts

1. The most common organizational structure for a narrative is

    A. cause and effect

    B. sequential

    C. problem-solution

    D. persuasive

Questions 2-4 refer to the following passage:

"Tom appeared on the sidewalk with a bucket of whitewash and a long-handled brush. He surveyed the fence, and all gladness left him and a deep melancholy settled down upon his spirit. Thirty yards of board fence nine feet high. Life to him seemed hollow, and existence but a burden. Sighing, he dipped his brush and passed it along the topmost plank; repeated the operation; did it again; compared the insignificant whitewashed streak with the far-reaching continent of unwhitewashed fence, and sat down on a tree-box discouraged."
    -From *The Adventures of Tom Sawyer* by Mark Twain

2. If a student were unfamiliar with the word "melancholy," which word(s) in the passage might provide the best context clue as to its meaning?

    A. "upon his spirit"

    B. "far-reaching"

    C. "insignificant"

    D. "gladness left him"

3. In this passage, Tom appears to be

    A. dedicated

    B. reluctant

    C. motivated

    D. inventive

4. The comparison of the "insignificant whitewashed streak" to the "far-reaching continent of unwhitewashed fence" is used to

    A. provide a precise measurement of the painted area

    B. demonstrate how hard Tom had been working

    C. emphasize the perceived enormity of Tom's task

    D. portray Tom as unintelligent

5. Identify the indirect object in the following sentence: "Maria loaned her book to Lauren."

    A. Maria

    B. loaned

    C. book

    D. Lauren

6. Which of these is NOT an example of a secondary source?

    A. A textbook

    B. An encyclopedia

    C. A research article

    D. An autobiography

7. The turning point of a story is known as the

    A. exposition

    B. conflict

    C. setting

    D. climax

8. Which of these behaviors does NOT demonstrate a deficit in concepts of print?

    A. Not reading words on a page from left to right

    B. Using a return sweep

    C. Attending only to pictures in a book and not the words

    D. Believing the story could change from one reading to the next

9. Which of the following would be the best topic sentence for a persuasive essay?

    A. World War II was a fight between the Axis and the Allies.

    B. World War II took place between 1939 and 1945.

    C. The use of the atomic bomb during World War II was not justified.

    D. New technologies were used in World War II.

10. Identify the error in the following sentences: "Maria moved to New York City last month. She lived in Brooklyn where she works in a café."

    A. Subject-verb agreement

    B. Tense agreement

    C. Ambiguous antecedent

    D. Punctuation

Question 11 refers to the following passage:

Whose woods these are I think I know.
His house is in the village, though;
He will not see me stopping here
To watch his woods fill up with snow.

My little horse must think it queer
To stop without a farmhouse near
Between the woods and frozen lake
The darkest evening of the year.

He gives his harness bells a shake
To ask if there is some mistake.
The only other sound's the sweep
Of easy wind and downy flake.

The woods are lovely, dark, and deep,
But I have promises to keep,
And miles to go before I sleep,
And miles to go before I sleep.
          —Robert Frost

11. The rhyme scheme for each of the first three stanzas of this poem can be described as

    A. ABAB

    B. AABB

    C. AABA

    D. ABCA

12. Changing "cat" to "bat" is an example of

    A. phoneme segmentation

    B. phoneme substitution

    C. phoneme identification

    D. phoneme blending

13. Which of these is considered an abstract noun?

    A. Donor

    B. Money

    C. Generosity

    D. Check

14. Which of the following types of writing should NOT include the author's personal opinion?

    A. Journaling

    B. Expository writing

    C. Poetry

    D. Persuasive writing

15. Which of the following is NOT considered a conjunction?

    A. But

    B. For

    C. At

    D. Or

16. The books an individual student reads should mostly fall under the category of

A. easy texts

B. frustration-level texts

C. just right texts

D. grade level texts

17. The purpose of an editorial is typically

A. to entertain

B. to inform

C. to persuade

D. to teach

18. Novels, short stories, and plays are common forms of

A. poetry

B. non-fiction

C. expository writing

D. narratives

19. Which of these singular nouns is NOT correctly paired with its plural form?

A. House - Houses

B. Mouse - Mouses

C. Box - Boxes

D. Ox - Oxen

20. Which of these language techniques tends to be the most difficult for many second language learners to understand?

A. Imagery

B. Idiom

C. Alliteration

D. Simile

21. By using a think-aloud while reading a text, a teacher promotes reading comprehension by

    A. demonstrating the process of text interaction

    B. discouraging metacognition

    C. asking students direct questions about the text

    D. providing background knowledge to enhance the understanding of a topic

22. "Lydia was feeling sick and dragged herself out of bed energetically." Which part of this sentence should be changed for it to make sense?

    A. Proper noun

    B. Adverb

    C. Action verb

    D. Preposition

23. Rhyming and segmenting are examples of

    A. phonological awareness skills

    B. concept of print

    C. decoding

    D. alphabetic principles

24. A diary is a(n)

    A. novel

    B. sonnet

    C. allegory

    D. primary source

25. "Manuscript," "transcription," and "descriptive" share a common

    A. prefix

    B. suffix

    C. end rhyme

    D. root word

26. A child who writes "I herd the anamuls make lots of noyz" is exhibiting which stage of writing development?

A. Conventional spelling

B. Random letters

C. Phonetic spelling

D. Letter-like forms

27. "Will you come to the party this weekend?" is an example of which type of sentence?

A. Interrogative

B. Exclamatory

C. Imperative

D. Declarative

28. Which of these words does NOT contain an affix?

A. Bicycle

B. Largest

C. Start

D. Prediction

29. Protagonist and antagonist are the two main types of

A. settings

B. conflicts

C. narrators

D. characters

30. Identify the antecedent in the following sentence: "Julia drank coffee while she worked on the report."

A. Julia

B. drank

C. she

D. report

31. "Because the forecast called for rain later in the day, I brought an umbrella with me." What type of sentence is this?

    A. Simple

    B. Compound

    C. Complex

    D. Compound-complex

32. Which of the following is NOT an appropriate way to correct a run-on sentence?

    A. Separate the two independent clauses with a semicolon.

    B. Separate the two independent clauses into two separate sentences.

    C. Join two independent clauses with a conjunction.

    D. Separate the two independent clauses with a comma.

33. Effective listening involves

    A. focusing on the speaker

    B. paying attention to nonverbal cues

    C. responding appropriately

    D. all of the above

34. In the writing process, which step follows revising?

    A. Publishing

    B. Creating a rough draft

    C. Editing

    D. Prewriting

35. Recognition of rhyme and print awareness are components of

    A. logographic foundation

    B. emergent literacy

    C. decoding

    D. fluency

36. "Teacher picked up book off of floor." This sentence is missing

    A. articles
    B. verbs
    C. prepositions
    D. nouns

37. "My daughter's doll" is an example of a(n)

    A. dependent clause
    B. independent clause
    C. phrase
    D. declarative sentence

38. The type of narrator that can explain the thoughts of any character is

    A. Omniscient
    B. First person
    C. Limited omniscient
    D. Second person

39. Which of the following words contains a consonant digraph?

    A. sublime
    B. house
    C. divergent
    D. graphic

40. Which of these is used NOT to measure fluency in reading?

    A. Accuracy
    B. Rate
    C. Flexibility
    D. Prosody

41. Identify the error in the following sentence: "George is a real estate agent and Tony is an insurance salesman. He has been with his company for ten years."

    A. Subject-verb agreement

    B. Ambiguous antecedent

    C. Capitalization

    D. Punctuation

42. Which of these skills is typically the first to develop?

    A. Syllabication

    B. Decoding

    C. Fluency

    D. Letter-sound correspondence

43. Mr. Brown assigns his class fifteen minute presentations on a research topic. Which of the following should his students do during their presentations in order to be as effective as possible?

    A. Read a prepared speech word for word

    B. Look directly at Mr. Brown throughout the presentation

    C. Make eye contact with various members of the audience

    D. Stand perfectly still

44. A question mark is most likely to be used in which type of sentence?

    A. Declarative

    B. Interrogative

    C. Imperative

    D. Exclamatory

45. Identify the error in the following sentence: "Lily and me went on vacation together."

    A. It is an independent clause.

    B. It is a dependent clause.

    C. It uses an object pronoun instead of a subject pronoun.

    D. It uses a subject pronoun instead of an object pronoun.

46. The understanding that words are made up of letters that have different sounds is known as

    A. phonemic awareness
    B. the alphabetic principle
    C. the logographic foundation
    D. syllabication

47. While speaking, Ms. King is looking for signs that her students are listening. Which of the following non-verbal cues gives the impression of effective listening?

    A. Maintaining eye contact with Ms. King
    B. Packing up supplies in backpacks
    C. Immediately raising a hand to ask a question while Ms. King is still speaking
    D. Putting heads down on desks

48. "Please pick up the book that's _____ the desk." What type of word would best complete this sentence?

    A. Preposition
    B. Conjunction
    C. Noun
    D. Adjective

49. In order to be considered a sentence, a group of words must at least contain

    A. a noun and a verb
    B. a noun and a conjunction
    C. a verb and a conjunction
    D. a noun and an adverb

50. Which of these does NOT contain meter?

    A. Blank verse
    B. Limerick
    C. Free verse
    D. Sonnet

51. In a primary election,

    A. each of the two major parties narrows the nominees down to one party candidate for president

    B. the president is selected by the people

    C. the votes are tallied and sent to the Electoral College

    D. rules and procedures are uniform across all states

52. A society that produces only what it needs for survival has a

    A. planned economy

    B. socialist economy

    C. subsistence economy

    D. open economy

53. Which of these Supreme Court cases had the most direct impact on race relations in the United States?

    A. *Marbury v. Madison*

    B. *Roe v. Wade*

    C. *Brown v. Board of Education*

    D. *Miranda v. Arizona*

54. The purpose of a(n) _____ is to carry out the day-to-day functions of a government.

    A. legislature

    B. bureaucracy

    C. judicial system

    D. executive

55. Which of these had the most direct influence on the adoption of the Thirteenth Amendment to the U.S. Constitution?

    A. The women's suffrage movement

    B. The end of Reconstruction

    C. Union victory in the Civil War

    D. Manifest Destiny

56. The United States' first attempt at a national government was

    A. the Constitution

    B. the Declaration of Independence

    C. the Articles of Confederation

    D. the Bill of Rights

57. The last half of the twentieth century in the United States was most shaped by

    A. disputes over the issue of slavery

    B. competition with the Soviet Union

    C. the desire for territorial expansion

    D. military conflict with Germany

58. The act of voting is an expression of the constitutional principle of

    A. popular sovereignty

    B. federalism

    C. separation of powers

    D. flexibility

59. Which of these was NOT a direct result of the Industrial Revolution in the United States?

    A. The population became more urbanized.

    B. Manufactured goods became more widely available and less expensive.

    C. Big businesses were subject to strict government regulations.

    D. Factories employed many immigrants for low wages.

60. Plantation farming was common in which colonial region?

    A. The South

    B. New England

    C. Mid-Atlantic

    D. Midwest

61. The New Deal was a response to

    A. severe economic downturn in the 1930s

    B. the pursuit of equal rights for African-Americans

    C. Soviet aggression during the Cold War

    D. the bombing of Pearl Harbor

62. Hawaii is an example of a(n)

    A. peninsula

    B. inlet

    C. archipelago

    D. country

63. Which of these was NOT one of the primary underlying causes for World War I?

    A. Imperialism

    B. Militarism

    C. Fascism

    D. Nationalism

64. Which of these primary sources would be most helpful to a student writing a report on the ratification of the U.S. Constitution?

    A. Common Sense by Thomas Paine

    B. The Declaration of Independence

    C. The Gettysburg Address

    D. The Federalist Papers by Alexander Hamilton, John Jay, and James Madison

65. Which of these terms refers to the limited nature of resources which drives economics?

    A. Surplus

    B. Scarcity

    C. Demand

    D. Tariff

66. Kevin is looking at a map of Pennsylvania and wants to know the distance from Philadelphia to Pittsburgh. Which of the following will he need to use?

    A. Compass rose

    B. Legend

    C. Scale

    D. Elevation

67. Tundra, alpine, and taiga are examples of

    A. biomes

    B. climates

    C. regions

    D. landforms

68. A student looking for the elevation of a mountain should use which type of map?

    A. Political

    B. Topographic

    C. Climate

    D. Historical

69. The Gadsden Purchase, the Mexican Cession, and the Louisiana Purchase were part of the United States'

    A. belief in Manifest Destiny

    B. New Deal programs

    C. 20th century imperialism

    D. Cold War era policy

Question 70 refers to the following passage:

"The history of the present King of Great Britain is a history of repeated injuries and usurpations, all having in direct object the establishment of an absolute tyranny over these States...

In every stage of these oppressions, we have petitioned for redress in the most humble terms: Our repeated petitions have been answered only by repeated injury. A prince whose character is thus marked by every act which may define a tyrant, is unfit to be the ruler of a free people...

We, therefore, the Representatives of the united States of America, in General Congress, Assembled, appealing to the Supreme Judge of the world for the rectitude of our intentions, do, in the name, and by authority of the good people of these Colonies, solemnly publish and declare, that these United Colonies are, and of right ought to be free and independent states; that they are absolved from all allegiance to the British Crown, and that all political connection between them and the State of Great Britain, is and ought to be totally dissolved."
–Second Continental Congress, 1776

70. At the time that it was written, which of the following would have been most likely to agree with the statements in this document?

    A. A loyalist
    B. A patriot
    C. A member of Parliament
    D. A monarch

71. The 1st Amendment includes all of the following EXCEPT

    A. freedom of speech
    B. the right to peacefully assemble
    C. the right to petition the government
    D. the right to bear arms

72. In a capitalist system, hard work is incentivized by

    A. the profit motive
    B. government demand
    C. guaranteed success
    D. subsidies

73. A topographic map would be most useful for

    A. calculating the population density of New York City

    B. finding the elevation of Beijing

    C. seeing how the borders of Poland have changed over time

    D. identifying the major agricultural products of France

74. The immediate cause of U.S. entry into World War II was

    A. the sinking of the Lusitania

    B. the Zimmerman telegram

    C. the use of the atomic bomb

    D. the bombing of Pearl Harbor

75. The rate of exchange describes

    A. the value of one nation's currency in relation to the currency of another nation

    B. the price a good or service will draw in the marketplace

    C. the balance of trade of a nation

    D. the cost of production for a good versus its sale price

Analysis

1. Your fourth grade class is reading *Charlie and the Chocolate Factory* by Roald Dahl, in which young Charlie Bucket wins the rare chance to tour a candy factory and meet its eccentric owner, Willy Wonka. As part of this unit, you have your students draw a new type of candy they would like to see sold by Wonka.

    I. Design and describe a writing activity to go along with the students' drawings

    II. Identify at least TWO specific writing skills that this activity would promote

_____
_____
_____
_____
_____
_____
_____
_____
_____
_____
_____
_____
_____
_____
_____
_____
_____
_____
_____
_____
_____
_____

2. You are teaching a unit to fifth grade students on the Civil War.

    I. Describe TWO specific ways you could integrate the study of geography into this unit.

Subtest II

Mathematics

1. Which of these units is NOT used to measure liquid volume?

A. pints

B. milliliters

C. grams

D. cups

2. There were 25 questions on a spelling test. If Kristen got 21 of them correct, what was her score expressed as a percentage?

A. 21%

B. 0.84

C. 0.96

D. 0.74

3. Tiling can be used to find the area of a

A. rectangle

B. circle

C. triangle

D. oval

4. The Pythagorean Theorem is used to find

A. the slope of a line

B. the volume of a cylinder

C. the sides of a right triangle

D. the midpoint of a line segment

5. A store buys t-shirts from the manufacturer in cases of 25 for $50. They sell the shirts for a price of $8 each. How much of a profit will the store make on the sale of 80 shirts?

A. $480

B. $640

C. $590

D. $30

6. What is the absolute value of -10?

    A. 10

    B. -10

    C. 1/10

    D. 1

7. The greatest common factor (GCF) of 15 and 18 is

    A. 3

    B. 90

    C. 5

    D. 18

8. The set {1, 4, 16, 64) is what type of sequence?

    A. Arithmetic

    B. Geometric

    C. Triangular

    D. Fibonacci

9. To solve $2(5 + 3)^2 - 10$, the first step would be to

    A. Multiply 2 by 5

    B. Square the 3

    C. Add 5 and 3

    D. Subtract 10

10. A student has the following word problem on a worksheet: "Jason is placing 6 cookies into bags to keep them fresh. If he puts 3 cookies in each bag, how many bags will he fill?" This question is an example of

    A. measurement division

    B. long division

    C. partitive division

    D. analytical division

11. For lunch on Wednesday, students have a choice of pizza or a peanut butter and jelly sandwich. For a drink, they can choose milk, chocolate milk, orange juice, or apple juice. How many combinations of main dishes and drinks are possible?

    A. 6
    B. 4
    C. 8
    D. 12

12. On a recent test, five friends had scores of 88, 92, 76, 94, and 80. What was their median score?

    A. 86
    B. 88
    C. 94
    D. 90

Question 13 refers to the diagram below.

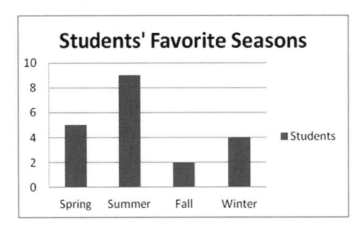

13. How many more students like summer than fall?

    A. 7.0
    B. 11.0
    C. 8.0
    D. 3.0

14. The school store sells notebooks and pencils. The ratio of sales today was 2 notebooks to 3 pencils. If the store sold 6 notebooks today, how many pencils did they sell?

    A. 3
    B. 9
    C. 6
    D. 12

15. 1, 4, 9, 16, 25... What is the next number in this sequence?

    A. 29
    B. 39
    C. 36
    D. 44

16. The area of a right triangle whose sides measure 3 cm, 5 cm, and 4 cm is

    A. 6
    B. 7.5
    C. 10
    D. 12

17. Which of the following is NOT considered a prenumeration concept?

    A. Pattern recognition
    B. Informal counting
    C. Relative magnitude
    D. Arithmetic operations

18. Which of these is considered an integer?

    A. .5
    B. -5
    C. 1/5
    D. 1.5

19. The measure of the angle that is supplementary to a 70° angle is
   A. 110°
   B. 20°
   C. -70°
   D. 30°

20. Line A contains the points (2, 4) and (4, 6). What is the slope of the line?
   A. 1
   B. 2
   C. -1
   D. 1/2

21. The product of two numbers is 12. The difference of these numbers is 4. What is the larger of the two numbers?
   A. 4
   B. 6
   C. 12
   D. 3

22. 2 is the only even number that is also
   A. rational
   B. prime
   C. natural
   D. irrational

23. Which of the following best illustrates the commutative property?
   A. 4 + 2 = 2 + 4
   B. (2 + 4) + 3 = 2 + (4 + 3)
   C. 2(4 + 3) = (2 * 4) + (2 * 3)
   D. 4 − 2 = 2 − 4

24. Which of these is NOT an equivalent ratio to the other three?

   A. one to three

   B. 1:3

   C. 2/6

   D. 3/1

25. Mrs. Nelson's class is 72% male. If there are 25 students in the class, how many students are females?

   A. 18

   B. 10

   C. 7

   D. 17

26. The multiples of 6 include

   A. 1, 2, and 3

   B. 3, 6, and 9

   C. 6, 12, and 18

   D. .6, 6, and 66

27. Which of theses in NOT equal to the other three?

   A. .25

   B. 25%

   C. 25

   D. 1/4

28. Put-together problems may contain an unknown

   A. product

   B. dividend

   C. addend

   D. divisor

29. Which of these numbers is the smallest in value?

    A. .39

    B. .317

    C. .3564

    D. .4

30. On a recent test, five friends had scores of 88, 92, 76, 94, and 80. What was the mean of their scores?

    A. 84

    B. 86

    C. 88

    D. 18

31. What is the least common multiple (LCM) of 4 and 5?

    A. 20

    B. 5

    C. 1

    D. 45

32. Two lines that never intersect are

    A. perpendicular

    B. complementary

    C. parallel

    D. supplementary

33. Which of these is NOT equivalent to 80 cm?

    A. 0.8 m

    B. 0.008 km

    C. 800 mm

    D. 80.0 cm

34. Which of these numbers is NOT equivalent to the others?

    A. 1/2

    B. 0.5

    C. 2/6

    D. 0.50

35. Solve for x. -4x < 16

    A. x > -4

    B. x < -4

    C. x < 4

    D. x > 4

36. One of the angles in an equilateral triangle has a measure of

    A. 90°

    B. 30°

    C. 60°

    D. 45°

37. If a car travels at 55 mph, how far will the car travel in 2 hours and 30 minutes?

    A. 140 miles

    B. 175 miles

    C. 12,650 miles

    D. 137.5 miles

38. The mean of a set is 15.6. The lowest value in the set is 10.2. The highest value in the set is 21.8. What is the absolute deviation of the highest value in the set?

    A. 6.2

    B. 11.6

    C. 5.4

    D. 2.6

39. To convert a mixed number to an improper fraction, _____ the denominator by the whole number and _____ the numerator.

A. multiply, add

B. divide, add

C. add, multiply

D. add, divide

40. Using a spinner with equal segments numbered 1-6, what is the probability of a spin landing on an even number?

A. 1/6

B. 1/3

C. 5/6

D. 1/2

Science

41. The food chain describes the

A. method of energy transfer through an ecosystem

B. ratio of producers to consumers in an ecosystem

C. way that food moves through the digestive system

D. nutritional value of basic food groups

42. A scientist reporting on the findings of an experiment should

A. omit the initial hypothesis if it proved untrue

B. give sufficient information for another scientist to replicate the results

C. present no original analysis of the data collected

D. not include areas for further investigation

43. An object's weight on Earth may be different than its weight on another planet. This is the result of

A. inertia

B. friction

C. gravity

D. normal force

44. Which of the following is NOT a characteristic of all living things?

A. Made of cells

B. Have definite life spans

C. Use energy

D. Sexual reproduction

45. In an ecosystems, top consumers transfer energy to

A. primary consumers

B. producers

C. decomposers

D. secondary consumers

46. The purpose of an experiment is to

A. test a hypothesis

B. collect measurement data

C. assess student learning

D. diagnose a problem

47. Meteorites are found

A. within the Earth's atmosphere

B. in the asteroid belt

C. near the sun

D. nowhere in this solar system

48. Which of these can disrupt the balance of an ecosystem?

A. Habitat destruction

B. Introduction of invasive species

C. Depletion of one species

D. All of the above

49. If two parents display the same recessive trait for eye color, the chances of the offspring also displaying the recessive trait are
    A. 0.0
    B. 0.25
    C. 0.75
    D. 1.0

50. The force present in a wire, cable, or cord when forces pull on both ends is known as
    A. normal force
    B. gravity
    C. tension force
    D. air resistance

51. Which part of a plant is responsible for reproduction?
    A. Stem
    B. Roots
    C. Leaves
    D. Flower

52. Which of these is ALWAYS true of an object in equilibrium?
    A. It is at rest.
    B. It is in motion.
    C. The resultant of all forces acting on the object is zero.
    D. It is subject only to normal force.

53. Which of these types of water movement in the water cycle does NOT involve a phase change?
    A. Melting
    B. Surface run-off
    C. Transpiration
    D. Evaporation

54. The phases of the Moon are most directly a result of

A. the Moon's rotation on its axis

B. the Moon's revolution around the Earth

C. Earth's revolution around the sun

D. the tilt of the Earth on its axis

55. Animal and plant cells both contain all of the following EXCEPT

A. mitochondria

B. chloroplasts

C. nucleus

D. cytoplasm

56. Which type of rock is formed by the cooling of magma?

A. Sedimentary

B. Igneous

C. Metamorphic

D. Cretaceous

57. Light emits

A. radiant energy

B. potential energy

C. nuclear energy

D. kinetic energy

58. The outermost layer of the Earth is called the

A. outer core

B. mantle

C. inner core

D. crust

59. The idea that an object in motion will stay in motion unless acted upon by an outside force is known as
   A. sublimation
   B. velocity
   C. inertia
   D. friction

60. Fission involves
   A. the joining of atomic nuclei
   B. the splitting of atomic nuclei
   C. the destruction of energy
   D. the creation of energy

61. Weather is most directly influenced by
   A. the rock cycle
   B. the water cycle
   C. the Moon
   D. Earth's rotation on its axis

62. The desire to satisfy curiosity and to find practical applications of scientific understandings are
   A. integrated process skills of engineering
   B. two of the primary motivations for scientific inquiry
   C. stages in the experiential learning process
   D. elements of the tentativeness of scientific knowledge

Health Education, Physical Education, and the Arts

63. In dramatic literature, a comedy is best described as
   A. a play whose main character meets an unfortunate ending
   B. a play without a central conflict
   C. a play that is funny
   D. a play with a happy ending for the main character

64. **Which of these is NOT considered a locomotor skill?**
    A. Running
    B. Throwing
    C. Sliding
    D. Skipping

65. **Shade and tint are primarily used in art to show**
    A. value
    B. shape
    C. form
    D. texture

66. **Which of these activities would best support the development of non-locomotor skills?**
    A. Galloping across the room
    B. Kicking a soccer ball into a goal
    C. Standing on one foot for one minute
    D. Dribbling a basketball

67. **In dance, which of these is NOT considered an element of space?**
    A. Direction
    B. Level
    C. Force
    D. Pathway

68. **In art, a line is defined as**
    A. a straight path that is infinite in both directions
    B. a pathway connecting two points
    C. the pathway of a moving point
    D. the outer edge of a two-dimensional work of art

69. The human body system responsible for the transport of blood is the

    A. repiratory system

    B. musculoskeletal system

    C. circulatory system

    D. nervous system

70. Tempo is most closely related to which element of music?

    A. Melody

    B. Texture

    C. Rhythm

    D. Volume

71. The common effects of stimulants include all of the following EXCEPT

    A. a high followed by a crash

    B. slowed responses

    C. irritability

    D. restlessness

72. Which of these is considered a form of drama?

    A. allegory

    B. puppetry

    C. novel

    D. parable

73. Which of these nutritional components contributes most to muscle growth?

    A. carbohydrates

    B. fat

    C. sodium

    D. protein

Question 74 refers to the following passage:

JULIET: (to Romeo) Good night, good night! parting is such
sweet sorrow,
That I shall say good night till it be morrow.
    -*Romeo and Juliet* by William Shakespeare, Act 2, Scene 2

74. The passage above is an example of

   A. monologue

   B. soliloquy

   C. dialogue

   D. prose

75. Which of the following helps reduce the risk of disease?

   A. Proper nutrition

   B. Vaccination

   C. Personal hygiene

   D. All of the above

Answers and Explanations

Subtest I

1. B

A sequential organization presents events in chronological order. The is the most common structure for a narrative.

2. D

"Gladness left him" proceeds "melancholy" and sets gladness up as the opposite of melancholy. As the gladness left, melancholy (sadness) took its place.

3. B

Tom is very discouraged by the prospect of painting the whole fence and is very reluctant to do so.

4. C

The comparison of how little fence Tom has painted compared with the unpainted fence ahead helps to show how large and daunting Tom found this task to be.

5. D

The indirect object is the one that is receiving the action of the verb. In this case, the book is being loaned TO Lauren, making her the indirect object.

6. D

An autobiography is a person's account of his or her own life, making it a primary source.

7. D

The climax of a story is where the conflict reaches a head and the story has its turning point.

8. B

A return sweep is going to the left side of a new line of text after finishing the line above. Using this correctly demonstrates an understanding of this concept of print.

9. C

A persuasive essay is one in which the author tries to convince the reader of a certain point of view. The only one of these sentences that expresses an opinion rather than a fact is C.

10. B

Tense should be consistent when talking about the same time period. "Moved," "lived," and "works" do not all maintain the same tense.

11. C

This poem contains end rhyme. In these stanzas, the last words of lines 1, 2, and 4 rhyme, while line 3 contains a different ending sound.

12. B

Phoneme substitution is an exercise in which one phoneme of a word is replaced with another phoneme to create a new word.

13. C

An abstract noun refers to an idea or concept rather than a concrete person, place, or object.

14. B

Expository writing is meant to be informative.

15. C

"At" is a preposition.

16. C

A "just right" text is a book that is not too easy for a student and provides a healthy amount of challenge without being so above the student's level that they are quickly driven to frustration. The level of a "just right" text varies with the individual student and may or may not align to what is considered "at grade level."

17. C

Editorials are opinion pieces and are a form of persuasive writing.

18. D

These are all examples of narratives, which tell a story.

19. B

The plural of "mouse" is "mice."

20. B

An idiom is a phrase that has come to have a different meaning through usage than the meanings of its individual words. Different languages have very different idioms and because it is difficult to ascertain the meaning of an idiom from the words it contains (without the prior cultural background knowledge), idioms can be particularly tricky for second language learners.

21. A

In a think-aloud, a teacher demonstrates his thinking process when reading a text, making comments and asking himself questions. This is a way to model the process for students.

22. B

The adverb "energetically" does not make sense with the rest of the sentence.

23. A

Phonological awareness is the understanding that words are made up of sound units. Rhyming and segmenting are two of its associated skills.

24. D

A diary is a type of primary source, which is a firsthand account of events from a person who witnessed them.

25. D

All of these share the common root "script" which means "write."

26. C

These words are written out like they sound (phonetically) instead of with correct spelling.

27. A

Interrogative sentences ask questions.

28. C

Affixes are prefixes and suffixes added to the beginning or end of base words to change their meaning.

29. D

A protagonist is the main character or hero. An antagonist works against the protagonist.

30. A

An antecedent is a noun for which a pronoun stands in. In this sentence, "she" is the pronoun, which refers to the antecedent "Julia."

31. C

A complex sentence contains one dependent and one independent clause.

32. D

Commas cannot be used to correct run-on sentences.

33. D

All of these actions are important components of active listening.

34. C

Revising is making changes to content. This step is followed by editing, which is correcting mechanical issues.

35. B

Emergent literacy refers to the language development that occurs before a child can read or write words. These skills are developed from birth and include listening, speaking, memory, recognizing pattern and rhyme, print awareness, critical thinking, and the development of the fine motor skills necessary for writing.

36. A

The sentence is missing articles such as "a" or "the."

37. C

Since this group of words contains no verb, it can only be classified as a phrase.

38. A

An omniscient narrator is able to describe the thoughts of any character. First person narration is in an "I" voice, while second person uses "you." Limited omniscient is a third person narrator who can only convey the inner thoughts of one character.

39. D

The "ph" in "graphic" is a consonant digraph because the two consonants combine to form a new sound.

40. C

Accuracy, rate, and prosody are all components of reading fluency. Flexibility is a component of mathematical (computational) fluency.

41. B

It is unclear from this sentence whether the pronoun "he" refers to George or Tony. This makes the antecedent ambiguous.

42. D

Letter-sound correspondence is the knowledge of the sounds that are associated with each letter of the alphabet. This is essential before any of the other skills can develop.

43. C

An important part of engaging an audience while speaking is making eye contact.

44. B

Interrogative sentences ask a question and end with a question mark.

45. C

The sentence should read "Lily and I went on vacation together."

46. B

The alphabetic principle is the understanding that words are made up of letters that have different sounds.

47. B

Eye contact helps a speaker to know that he or she has the audience members' focus.

48. A

This sentence requires a preposition such as "on" or "under."

49. A

A sentence must contain a noun and a verb.

50. C

Free verse poetry contains neither rhyme nor meter.

51. A

For many offices, the major parties hold primary elections (typically in the spring preceding the general election) in which voters choose who among a pool of candidates will become the official candidate for the party. The winning candidates from each party then face off against one another in the general election in November.

52. C

A subsistence economy is one in which the people produce only what they need to survive.

53. C

Brown v. Board of Education made the long-standing policy of "separate but equal" segregation illegal and was a major step forward in the movement for equal rights for African-Americans.

54. B

A bureaucracy is the organizational structure of a government containing the employees and mechanisms that carry out the daily functions of the government.

55. C

The Thirteenth Amendment abolished slavery and was adopted soon after the Civil War.

56. C

The newly formed United States created its first government under the Articles of Confederation. It was ineffective and later replaced by the Constitution.

57. B

From the end of World War II until the dissolution of the Soviet Union in 1991, United States foreign policy was primarily driven by its Cold War competition with the Soviet Union.

58. A

Popular sovereignty is the right of the people to rule through voting.

59. C

Big business was fairly unregulated in the 19th century, which led to much abuse. Regulations to protect consumers were put into place in the 20th century.

60. A

Due to the warm climate and rich soil, agriculture thrived in the Southern colonies and large-scale plantation farming became common.

61. A

The New Deal was President Franklin D. Roosevelt's domestic program designed to help the economy recover during the Great Depression of the 1930s.

62. C

Hawaii is an archipelago—a chain of islands.

63. C

Fascist regimes came to power in Europe after World War I and their rise was a cause of World War II.

64. D

The Federalist Papers were written in order to persuade people to support ratification.

65. B

Scarcity of resources means that resources are limited. How limited supplies of resources are to be allocated is foundational to economics.

66. C

Scale is used to show how distances on a map compare to real-life distances.

67. A

Biomes are large areas that have distinct sets of plant and animal life that are well-adapted to the environment. Biomes are classified according to geography and climate.

68. B

Elevation (how high land is above sea level) is shown on a topographic map.

69. A

Manifest Destiny was the belief that the United States should extend from the Atlantic to the Pacific. These territorial acquisitions helped the nation to reach that goal.

70. B

A patriot (a supporter of the American Revolution) would have supported this document, the Declaration of Independence.

71. D

The right to bear arms is in the 2nd Amendment.

72. A

The idea that one's hard work and innovation can pay off through increased profits is a motivating factor in a capitalist system.

73. B

Topographic maps are physical maps that show elevation.

74. D

The United States entered World War II on the side of the Allies after Japan, an Axis power, bombed the U.S. naval base at Pearl Harbor, Hawaii in 1941.

75. A

The monetary system of a particular nation is known as a currency. Currencies have different values in relation to one another, which are expressed as a rate of exchange.

Analysis Section: Sample Constructed-Response Answers

1. *After the students drew their pictures of the candy they have designed, I would have the students write letters to Willy Wonka telling him about their candy idea and asking him to make and sell it. In their letters, students would have to provide a detailed description of the candy and state the reasons that Willy Wonka should make and sell it. This would promote several writing skills. First, students would have to use the proper formatting for a letter. It would also require them to practice using descriptive language as they detail their creations to Willy Wonka. Finally, this exercise would develop their skills in persuasive writing as they would have to craft a compelling argument for Wonka to make and sell the candy, convincing him of its merits and that people would want to buy it.*

2. *I could integrate geography into the unit as we discussed the issue of the balance of slave and free states in the period leading up to the Civil War by having students fill in a map of the United States, coloring and labeling the free and slave states and their dates of admission. As we moved on to the war itself, I could have the students map the major battles of the Civil War and chart the progression of the Union and Confederate troops.*

Subtest II

1. C

Grams are used to measure mass.

2. B

21/25 * 100 = 84

3. A

Tiling- splitting a shape into unit squares- can be used to find the area of a rectangle with whole-number side lengths. None of the other shapes listed could be split evenly into unit squares.

4. C

The Pythagorean Theorem is $a^2 + b^2 = c^2$, where a and b are the lengths of the legs of a right triangle and c is the length of the hypotenuse.

5. A

If 25 shirts cost $50 from the manufacturer, the cost per shirt is $2. For 80 shirts, the cost would be $160. The sale price per shirt is $8, which comes to $640 for 80 shirts. Profit = price - cost. $640 - $160 = $480

6. A

Absolute value is a number's distance from zero and is always a positive number.

7. A

The factors of 15 are 1, 3, 5, and 15. The factors of 18 are 1, 2, 3, 6, 9, and 18. The greatest common factor is 3.

8. B

To get from one member of the set to the next, multiply by 4. A set whose rule is solely multiplication is called a geometric set.

9. C

The first step in the order of operations is to take care of operations within parentheses.

10. A

Measurement division is needed when students know how many objects are in each group but do not know how many groups there are.

11. A

You can solve this problem by drawing a tree diagram of the possibilities, by listing out the possible combinations, or by using multiplication. 2 choices for sandwiches multiplied by 3 choices for drinks equals 6 possible combinations.

12. B

To find the median, put the scores in numerical order. The median is the number is the middle. In order, the numbers read: 76, 80, 88, 92, 94. The number in the middle is 88.

13. A

9 students like summer the best and 2 students like fall the best. 9 − 2 = 7

14. B

Solve by setting up a proportion.

15. C

This is a set of perfect squares.

16. A

The formula for the area of a triangle is A =1/2 bh. In this case, the triangle is right so the two shorter sides will represent the base and the height. (The longest side in a right triangle is always the hypotenuse.) 1/2 * 3 * 4 = 6

17. D

Prenumeration concepts are elements of math-related reasoning that a child develops prior to any formal mathematical knowledge. These include all of the choices listed, except for algebraic operations, which is a true mathematical concept that must be taught.

18. B

Integers are numbers that do not contain fractional parts (whole numbers and their negatives).

19. A

Supplementary angles add up to 180°.

20. A

The slope formula is $m = (y_2 - y_1)/(x_2 - x_1)$

21. B

The two numbers are 6 and 2. 6 * 2 = 12 and 6 - 2 = 4.

22. B

A prime number can only be divided evenly by itself and 1. 2 is the only even number that is prime because every other even number can be divided by 2.

23. A

The commutative property states that in a multiplication or addition problem, the order of the numbers being added or multiplied does not affect the final result.

24. D

3/1 represents a ratio of 3 to 1, not 1 to 3. 2/6 is a fraction equivalent to 1/3, so it also is an equivalent ratio.

25. C

72% of 25 is 18 (25 * 0.75 = 18). That means there are 18 males in the class. To find out how many females there are, subtract the number of males from the total.

26. C

Multiples are the result of multiplying a number by positive integers. 6 * 1 = 6; 6 * 2 = 12;   6 * 3 = 18; etc.

27. C

.25, 25%, and 1/4 are all equivalent.

28. C

Addition can be modeled as a "put-together" problem, with either an unknown addend or an unknown sum.

29. B

When comparing decimals, move from left to right. A, B, and C all have a 3 in the tenths place. In the hundredths place, choice B has a 1, which is the smallest of the given values.

30. B

To find the mean, add up the scores and divide by the number of scores (5).

31. A

The only one of these choices that is a multiple of 4 and 5 is 20.

32. C

Lines that never touch are parallel. Perpendicular lines intersect at a right angle. The terms complimentary and supplementary refer to angles, not lines.

33. B

80 cm = 0.0008 km

34. C

2/6 is equal to 1/3. All of the other choices are equal to 1/2.

35. A

Remember to switch the inequality sign when dividing each side by a negative number.

36. C

All sides and angles of a triangle are equal therefore each angle in an equilateral triangle must equal 60°.

37. D

Convert 2 hours and 30 minutes to 2.5 hours. 55 miles per hour multiplied by 2.5 hours equals 137.5 miles.

38. A

Absolute deviation is the distance of a number in a set from the mean. 21.8 - 15.6 = 6.2

39. A

To convert a mixed number to an improper fraction, multiply the denominator by the whole number and add the numerator.

40. D

The even numbers in this set are 2, 4, and 6. That means that there are 3 favorable outcomes out of 6 possible outcomes. The probability of getting an even number is 3/6, which reduces to 1/2.

41. A

The food chain shows how energy gets from producers (plants) that make energy to consumers (animals) that get the energy through eating plants and other animals.

42. B

A good experiment should be able to be replicated by another scientist, yielding the same results. This would help to verify the original scientist's findings.

43. C

Gravity, the force that pulls smaller objects toward a much larger one, such as a planet, is what is responsible for weight. Weight varies on different planets due to different levels of gravitational pull.

44. D

Some organisms use sexual reproduction, while others utilize asexual reproduction.

45. D

A top consumer is an animal that is at the top of the food chain, meaning it is not prey for any other animal. When the animal dies, its energy will be transferred to decomposers who process the dead tissue and return it to the Earth.

46. A

Experiments are used to verify known scientific facts or to test new hypotheses.

47. A

"Meteorite" is the name given to meteoroids once they enter Earth's atmosphere.

48. D

Any of these factors can disrupt the delicate balance of any ecosystem.

49. D

For a recessive trait to be displayed, the offspring must have two genes for the recessive trait. If both parents have only recessive genes, the offspring will also have the recessive genes.

50. C

Tension force is the force present in a wire, cable, or cord when forces pull on both ends.

51. D

The flower is the site of reproduction in plants.

52. C

Equilibrium is achieved when the resultant of all forces acting on an object is zero. This means that the object could either be at rest or in unaccelerated motion.

53. C

In surface run-off, water remains in liquid form. Run-off occurs when the soil becomes oversaturated with water and the excess comes to the surface and flows over land.

54. B

The Moon takes 28 days to revolve around the Earth, during which time its position determines how it will appear from Earth and gives it distinct phases.

55. B

Only plant cells contain chloroplasts, which are the site of photosynthesis.

56. B

Igneous rock is formed when magma cools and hardens.

57. A

Radiant energy is the energy of electromagnetic waves such as light.

58. D

The crust is the surface of the Earth on which life exists.

59. C

The idea that an object in motion will stay in motion and an object at rest will stay at rest unless acted upon by an outside force is known as inertia. This is part of Newton's First Law of Motion.

60. A

Fission is the splitting of atoms. Fission is the type of reaction used to create atomic bombs and nuclear reactors.

61. B

The water cycle is responsible for precipitation, which is a major component of weather.

62. B

There are many reasons that people undertake scientific inquiry. Two of the major motivations for scientific exploration are a desire to satisfy curiosity about the world and seeking practical applications of science that will benefit humanity.

63. D

In drama, comedies are plays that result in a happy ending for the main character. They are usually light-hearted, but not always funny. Comedies are the opposite of tragedies, wherein the main character has an unhappy ending, often as a consequences of his own choices.

64. B

Locomotor skills involve travelling movement from place to place. Throwing is considered a manipulative skill because it involves the use of equipment.

65. A

Value is the lightness or darkness of a shape. Shades are darker in value and tints are lighter.

66. C

Standing on one foot helps develop balance, which is a non-locomotor skill.

67. C

Force is the energy used to create motion in dance. Space is the area in which the dance takes place. Direction (which way the movement is going), level (how high off the ground the movement is occurring), and pathway (the path the movement takes) are all elements of space.

68. C

In art, a line is any pathway created by a moving point. It does not necessariliy have to be straight, like it does in math.

69. C

The circulatory system transports blood throughout the human body through veins and arteries.

70. C

Tempo is the speed of a piece of music and is related to rhythm.

71. B

Slowed responses are a common effect of depressants.

72. B

Puppetry is a form of drama usually intended for a children's audience. It uses dialogue to convey the story.

73. D

Protein helps to build muscle.

74. C

In this scene from a play by William Shakespeare, one character is speaking directly to another. This is called dialogue.

75. D

All of these help to prevent the spread of disease.

Made in the USA
Columbia, SC
02 June 2019